WEEKEND Refresh

WEEKEND
Refresh

Home Design in 48 Hours or Less

TASTEMADE

Clarkson Potter/Publishers
New York

Published in the United States by
Clarkson Potter/Publishers, an imprint
of Random House, a division of
Penguin Random House LLC, New York.
ClarksonPotter.com
RandomHouseBooks.com

CLARKSON POTTER is a trademark
and POTTER with colophon is a
registered trademark of
Penguin Random House LLC.

Library of Congress Cataloging-in-
Publication Data
Names: Tastemade (Firm), editor.
Title: Weekend refresh : home design
in 48 hours or less / Tastemade.
Description: New York : Clarkson
Potter, [2023] | Includes index. |
Identifiers: LCCN 2022015486 (print)
| LCCN 2022015487 (ebook) | ISBN
9780593232866 (hardcover) | ISBN
9780593232873 (ebook) Subjects:
LCSH: Housekeeping. | House
furnishings—Design and construction.
| Interior decoration accessories—
Design and construction. | Interior
decoration. | Do-it-yourself work.
Classification: LCC TX301 .W44 2023
(print) | LCC TX301 (ebook) | DDC
648—dc23/eng/20220803

LC record available at https://lccn
.loc.gov/2022015486 LC ebook
record available at https://lccn.loc
.gov/2022015487

ISBN 978-0-593-23286-6
Ebook ISBN 978-0-593-23287-3

Printed in China

Creative Direction: Brenna Darling,
Lily Ng, and Megahn Perry
Writer: Brenna Darling
Project Oversight: Tyler Wildermuth,
Daniel Kesner, and Jeremy Strauss
Photographer: Bethany Nauert
Photography Styling: Brenna Darling
Photography Assistants: Erika
Hokanson, David Klaus, and
David Dailey
Artists: Carla Llanos, Cameron
Stevens, Dominique Vari, Heather Que,
Helen Pasternak, and Mikayla Lapierre
Editor: Angelin Adams
Editorial Assistant: Darian Keels
Designer: Jennifer K. Beal Davis
Production Editor: Patricia Shaw
Production Manager: Kelli Tokos
Compositor: Merri Ann Morrell
Copy Editor: Diana Drew
Indexer: Cathy Dorsey
Marketer: Samantha Simon
Publicist: Natalie Yera

Cover design by Jennifer K. Beal Davis
Cover photographs by Bethany Nauert

10 9 8 7 6 5 4 3 2 1

First Edition

This book is dedicated to our crafty Tastemade Home community, whose desire to create a well-loved home inspires us daily.

CONTENTS

Introduction

Welcome to *Weekend Refresh*. This isn't *just* a gorgeous coffee table book for you to ooh and aah over; this is the kind of book that will literally teach you how to redesign and repurpose that very same coffee table, using the right techniques and tools, instead of just making it look pretty. We believe that home design is for everyone, and that means you (yes, YOU!) can do every project we lay out in this book. The best part? Each one can be done in 48 hours. Let us help you turn any room into a well-designed space.

When Tastemade Home began, we pretty much knew right away that our goal would be to showcase accessible design and empower people to make their spaces a reflection of themselves. The founders of Tastemade—Larry Fitzgibbon, Joe Perez, and Steven Kydd—wanted to bring together a community of Tastemakers who are passionate about food, travel, and design, and, by doing so, change the way the world watches and engages with online content. Here at Tastemade, we strive to encourage our audience to make incredible meals *and* have a beautifully decorated space to serve them in. Our *Weekend Refresh* series was born from that very idea; home design shouldn't just be aspirational. Whether you're a renter, living in a small space, a new homeowner, or on a budget, your home should make you feel good. Personalized, intentional, and well-thought-out décor can help do that.

To *refresh* is to make over your space. We hope we inspire you to pick up those power tools and make something incredible. There are endless ways to flex those crafty muscles and we are here to be your biggest cheerleaders. When you roll up your sleeves and put a little (okay, sometimes a lot) of elbow grease into a project, your home starts to morph into an oasis. There's no pressure to get it all done at once—a beautiful home takes time! Pick a room and find a project, and in 48 hours you'll have a brand-new space. Next weekend move right along to your next two-day transformation. Be advised . . . DIY can become addictive. Sorry, not sorry!

As you progress through your home, your skills will improve, and your confidence will skyrocket. No one starts out as an expert, despite how social media makes it look. Start small and paint one wall before jumping into the proverbial DIY

pond headfirst. Or do the total opposite, if that's more your speed, and learn by trial and error. There is no "correct" way to design and decorate. Sure, we have some suggestions, like when in doubt consider styling shelves in groups of three and make sure you measure and map out furniture before buying. But, for the most part, we think hard-and-fast rules are made to be broken. You do you and make your space a reflection of what feels right.

Our homes tell the stories of our lives, and no two lives are the same. Let's get ready to refresh!

page 162

HOW TO USE THIS BOOK

Look to this book not only when you're in need of inspiration, but also when you're in need of instruction. Not only are we going to teach you how to redo spaces, but we'll also teach you how to enjoy and maintain them over time. Whether you're a first-time homeowner, a renter, or a DIY-aholic, our goal is to show you how to refresh your home, one weekend at a time.

Before we get started on any projects, we will walk you through *how* to get started. We have suggestions for some of the essential tools you'll need to get your toolbox up to snuff. The good news here is that your toolbox will be ever-evolving and growing—start with the basics and

add to it as needed on a project-by-project basis. You'll notice that a lot of the 101s in this book use the same tools, and each will have the necessary ones noted right at the top. How easy is that? Next, we'll guide you in making a moodboard, which is a visual preparation step that is just as important as having the right equipment. We want you to look at the overall form and function of the space presented and decide what works for you. It's something we always do at Tastemade that helps to get our refreshes on the right track, right away.

Now that your tool kits—both literal and mental—are properly prepped, let's get started. In part one, we focus on upgrading your space. We have the book laid out just as you'd walk into and through a house, starting with curb appeal and the entrance, then going through each room. We'll address some common scenarios that could present roadblocks when coming up with a design. Along the way, we'll point out ways to personalize and customize your space, from your entryway to your backyard and everything in between. In each room, we'll draw attention to particular projects, which we call "101s." These are projects that we've done ourselves—and are even featured in some of our *Weekend Refresh* episodes! They will help you learn, step-by-step, the specific things you can accomplish at home. There is a range in difficulty (levels 1 through 3), which you'll see noted at the beginning of each project. Feeling a little nervous about getting started? Find a level 1 project and build up your confidence. Feeling more ambitious? Go for a level 3. We believe that you can do every single project in this book, no matter what your experience level is.

Once you've gotten your home to look the way you want, it's time to focus on the way it makes you feel. In part two, we want you to get in there! With our "Guide to Being a Good Plant Parent," we explore the best indoor and outdoor plants for your space with tips on watering, good light conditions, and general plant care. We want you to feel good in your space and have the friends and family who visit your home to feel great, too. Keeping organized and maximizing storage space is so important to being a rock-star host. From 101s that set the mood for a killer party, to projects that will make your guests

feel welcome, you have everything you need to maximize the enjoyment of your home. Entertaining should be stress-free, so we guarantee that all our 101s can be completed within our 48-hour refresh timeline. You'll spend less time with setup and more time making memories with the people you care about.

You've done all the work to refresh your space, maybe you've had the chance to throw an epic bash—and do we spy a plant or two being beautifully taken care of? In part three, we give you pointers on how best to maintain your home, from cleaning to repairs. We have handy-dandy laundry tips on getting out stains using ordinary household products. There's also a cleaning chart that we hope makes cleaning less intimidating and breaks up tasks by day, month, and season. If you do a little bit at a time, rather than a whole lot every blue moon, maintaining your home will become a lot more manageable. Part three will be your one-stop shop for all the questions you would normally call your mom about. We promise that "boring" things can be fun when you have the right knowledge at your fingertips.

Throughout the book, read our "Life Hacks" for hints about how to work smarter not harder. We hope these little nuggets of info help make your weekend refreshes fly by with ease and make each 101 even more fun. Remember: All you need are the right tools and the belief that you are worthy of living in a beautiful space. For what it's worth, we believe in you.

Happy refreshing!

page
166

Tool Kit

For every project you undertake, you need the right tools.
You can't do it alone!

Think of buying each tool as an investment. You buy a hammer once, and you'll most likely have it for years to come. Start with these basics as a solid foundation, and build your tool kit up from there, one at a time. A beginner refresher probably won't need a tile saw . . . so skip the fancy tools until you graduate to a more advanced-DIY status.

Tool storage is important, too. Get on with your bad self and purchase a legit toolbox. You'll feel like a total pro, you'll be able to cart your tools easily, and you'll know exactly where your tools are when you start your next project. Store your toolbox in a dry place, as moisture in the air can rust any metal parts. A tool belt is also super handy when doing projects around the home. Dress for success, and success will follow!

Before you dig into this book, make sure you have these key tools in your home. At the beginning of each 101, we have the necessary tools all listed, so you can begin knowing that you're covered each step of the way.

- Brad nailer + brads
- Circular saw
- Command strips
- Cutting brush
- Cutting shears
- Foam roller
- Gorilla Glue (not for hair)
- Hammer, screwdriver + chisel
- Small electric sander + sandpaper in various grits
- Jigsaw
- Level
- Measuring tape (analog or digital *with lasers—fun!*)
- Nails, screws (various sizes) + wall anchors
- Paint tray + drop cloth
- Paint-can opener
- Painter's tape + smoother tool
- Pencil + marking chalk
- Power drill + drill bits
- Sawhorses
- Staple gun + staples
- Stud finder
- Work gloves
- X-Acto knife, scissors + wire snips
- At least two deliveries of stuffed-crust pizza. (You're going to need lunch.)

LIFE HACK: REFRESH OUTFITS
Have a few designated "refresh" outfits that you don't mind getting dirty. Trust us, you don't want to ruin your favorite jeans by accidentally leaning on wet paint mid-project . . . Coveralls are a great, durable option that make any refresher look legit.

SAFETY FIRST

From operating power tools to properly protecting yourself while painting, it's important to stay safe during all projects. We want you to have the best refresh experience possible! Here are some basic rules to follow:

1. Always wear a mask, work gloves, and safety goggles when cutting or sanding wood. The mask helps keep you from breathing in wood shavings and dust; the gloves keep your fingers safe from potential splinters; and the safety goggles keep your eyes safe from any flying debris. Also, consider hearing protection when using loud tools.

2. Clamps are a great investment for securing wood while using power tools, like a jigsaw or a circular saw. They're kind of like an extra set of hands! Look for midrange clamps in a variety of sizes so you have what you need for all sorts of projects.

3. Close-toed shoes are a MUST when working on any kind of construction site. Leave the sandals and flip-flops for the beach.

4. Open windows to properly ventilate when painting. If you're in a small space or pregnant, wear a respirator and keep fans on.

5. Have a first-aid kit stocked and nearby. Include basic items like a variety pack of adhesive bandages, roller bandages, medical tape, antiseptic wipes, sterile gauze, and burn ointment.

6. Read instruction manuals when operating new tools. Remember to unplug them before making any adjustments, like switching drill bits or adding fresh sandpaper.

7. Clean as you go to keep a neat workspace and avoid any tripping hazards. Plus, it will be easier to pack up when you're done!

8. For all outdoor projects, we recommend wearing a solid pair of work gloves to protect your hands and make it easier to handle tough materials.

Moodboards

Oh, how we love them!

The first step to designing a space is designing that space on paper (or digitally!). The planning phase is crucial to curating a cohesive home that feels like YOU. The biggest tip to keep in mind during this part of the process is to Take. Your. Time. It's so tempting to rush out and start buying pretty things, but this often results in a chaotic aesthetic. We will get to the shopping and refreshing—promise! But without a clear picture in your mind of the direction you're headed in, you might end up wasting time and money.

How do you want your space to look? How do you want it to function? And how do you want to feel when you're in it?

A moodboard is a collection of images, colors, and inspiration that help you mix and match your design elements before you jump into your project. A solid moodboard makes for a solidly designed space. Your moodboard should get you excited about your home and

moodboards are so much fun to make!

LIFE HACK: VISUALIZING YOUR UPDATES

If you're more of a kinesthetic thinker, go out and buy some magazines and tear out the photos that inspire you. It's like old-fashioned Pinterest! You may have limited resources, based on the number of magazines you purchase, but you will be able to instantly visualize what your space will look like.

Before the moodboard comes the pinning—if you haven't done this already, Pinterest will be your new best friend. Seek out and follow designers you admire to see what they're working on or what *they're* pinning. There are no rules when it comes to Pinterest-ing for your project, but we do recommend keeping a few things in mind. First, you're not limited to pins of living rooms if you're refreshing your living room. Pin everything in sight that makes you feel alive or gives you a tingle of inspiration. Does an ocean sunrise make you feel calm and serene? This could tell you that your design eye leans toward California casual. Maybe androgenous fashion is making your stomach flip over with joy, perhaps indicating that you like clean lines and minimalist design. If you're drawn toward pictures of plants all day, every day, it shows you that you might love a bohemian aesthetic. This all informs the type of space you want to be in.

Second, go back and look at your board after a few days with an objective eye. Are you gravitating toward neutrals or bright, vibrant spaces? Is a similar color showing up in multiple images? Does a specific material, like wood, metal, or velvet, pop up throughout your images? This will help you home in on the type of vibe you're going for and give you the springboard for the rest of the project.

Now that your style is curated, you are READY to make an epic moodboard. For example, you've pinned multiple images of a metal four-poster bed. You are leaning toward that type of bed for a reason, so begin your search for where to actually purchase one. You may find the *exact* one that makes your heart flutter, so screen-grab that image and insert it directly into your moodboard. That's one decision made with finality, and you can then build the rest of the room around it. Paint colors are a great place to start when envisioning a room. You should physically *go* to the hardware store to pick up a few paint chips to help make your decision. Colors look a lot different in person than they do online so it's wise to paint a sample swatch on the wall of your room to see how the specific lighting of your home affects the color. Once you pick the perfect one, add that image to your moodboard. Other things to include are textiles, art that inspires you, screen-grabs of furniture you love, and potential lighting choices. Once you add all these images together on one moodboard, you can start to visualize your space and ensure that everything dovetails nicely with your dream aesthetic.

Here are some ways to make them, and some examples of great moodboards:

PHOTOSHOP

Pros: Endless creative options on layering images, quick to use once you learn how, tons of online tutorials, advanced editing capabilities, professional presentation, and numerous transfer options.

Cons: Steep learning curve/ complicated when you first start out, expensive software.

SLIDE SHOW

Pros: Intuitive and user-friendly, free (typically preinstalled on most devices), drag + drop to manipulate images, copy + paste images from the internet, each slide can represent a different room.

Cons: Multiple steps to remove white backgrounds from images, less flexibility, fewer online "help" videos.

Living Room
Moodboard

POSTER BOARD AND GLUE

Pros: Physical visualization of your room, fun to craft with your hands, lets you incorporate a variety of materials (not just images).

Cons: Limited to images found in magazines, time-consuming, potentially messy.

LIFE HACK: KEEP YOUR MOODBOARD HANDY

Always keep your moodboard readily available when making design decisions, like picking out textiles, décor, or paint colors. It's easy to be swayed by pretty store displays, but that doesn't always mean that what you see in the store will work in the space you planned. It's great to have a reminder of your vision to keep you on track. And if you do want to shift gears mid-project, then you'll know it was an informed, thought-out decision.

PART 1:

Upgrade Your Space

Okay, you've got the tools, you've got the moodboard. Let's get to the makeover.

You can accomplish a lot in one weekend, especially since you've now taken the time to hone your design aesthetic and curate a dream home moodboard. Remember: Trends in the design world come and go, but, ultimately, trust your taste and the things you are drawn to. It will make you spend smarter as you refresh and love the result that much more. We'll start at the beginning, right at the curb of your home, and walk you through each room, all the way to the backyard. The possibilities are endless when it comes to how your home can work for you, but, at the end of the day, it should just make you happy to be there.

To us, upgrading your space doesn't have to include knocking down walls or gutting your house. You'd be amazed by what the power of paint, a few projects, and a well-thought-out vision can do for your home. The 101s in this section are meant to help you maximize what you already own, on top of showcasing your unique design aesthetic. They are the building blocks to help you complete fun projects with your roommates, partners, or families. Adjust the suggested paint colors, patterns, or plants to fit your style. (Feel free to flip ahead to our "Guide to Being a Good Plant Parent" on page 170 for indoor or outdoor plant ideas—we won't mind!) That is the cool thing about DIY and refreshing—it's totally customizable. Don't forget to share your progress online with the Tastemade community. We love seeing what our audience comes up with. Who doesn't love a good Before and After?

page
33

page
30

page
26

Entrances & Entryways

Entrances and entryways are the welcome sign for the rest of your house. Take a walk around the exterior of your house and make some decisions about what you want to see when you walk in the door and what you want others to know about you. It's not just about throwing your keys on a hook; it's about escaping from the outside world and transitioning into what should be the very best of YOU.

Do you ever drive around during the holidays and smile at all the care and cheer emanating from your neighborhood? Wouldn't it be great to capture that same essence all year round? We're not saying keep the holiday décor up for 12 months but it should always be a joy to pull up to your home. Curb appeal has a lot to do with that. What exactly *is* curb appeal? Basically, it's anything on the property you see from the street, like the landscaping, front entrance, and paint color. When you're a renter, there aren't many permanent changes you can make, but that doesn't mean you can't maximize your home's curb appeal.

Think about what would make you feel most welcome when walking up to your own home, then set aside 48 hours to make it happen.

CREATING AN ENTRANCE WITH PLANTS & OBJECTS

MATERIALS

- outdoor broom
- 1 large planter (22" to 25" tall)
- 1 medium planter (15" to 17" tall)
- 1 small planter (10" to 12" tall)
- rocks
- potting soil
- plants to fill the planters
- various outdoor décor objects
- welcome mat

Nothing says welcome home like a beautiful front door area to greet you. If you start with a solid decor base, then you can have fun adding or subtracting your exterior decor by seasons or holidays. It doesn't matter if you have a small stoop, or a wraparound porch. Your entrance can feel like an extension of the interior. Follow along to create an inviting entrance!

Step 1: Thoroughly sweep your front entrance using an outdoor broom—get all the cobwebs and dust out of any nooks and crannies. It's always good to start with a clean slate.

Step 2: Place a large, medium, and small planter to one side of the door. Fill the bottoms with small rocks to help with drainage (planters with drainage holes at the bottom are ideal). Next, add a layer of potting soil to each planter. Pick plants that fit your aesthetic (for example, manicured topiaries are perfect for a traditional décor style, while Boston ferns suit a boho vibe), and place one in each planter. Use the same plants for the same-size planters for a uniform look. Pack in more potting soil around the edges to secure your plants, and water according to your plants' needs.

Step 3: Add your house number in a clearly visible and unique way, like the "House Number Planter Box" on page 33.

Step 4: Add various outdoor décor objects, like a metal lantern or a sculpture, making it a grouping of three total objects. Visually, groups of three and odd numbers look appealing.

Step 5: Add a welcome mat, like the DIY "Floral Explosion Welcome Mat" on page 30.

Step 6: From here, add holiday décor, depending on the season!

LIFE HACK: MAKING DRAINAGE HOLES
To add drainage holes to planters, use a drill with a ¼" drill bit. Turn the planter upside down and slowly press the drill into the center of the bottom until it pops through and creates a hole. Add additional holes for larger pots!

PAINTING YOUR FRONT DOOR

MATERIALS

- painter's tape
- cutting brush
- quality exterior paint
- foam roller brush

Here's your first opportunity to introduce yourself to the neighborhood, so choose a color that both represents you and complements your home. Plus, painting a door is an easy way to upgrade your entrance. If you have a screen or storm door, go ahead and paint the frame for a seamless look. Don't be afraid to make the color really POP.

Step 1: Using your painter's tape, tape off any windows or glass that you don't want to get paint on. Tape off adjacent siding as well. Tape off existing hardware (knobs and hinges). If you're planning on changing the hardware (see "Door Hardware Upgrade" on page 29), remove the old knobs before painting. BTW—prepping for paint always takes twice as long as the painting itself, but don't skip this step! Proper prep leads to a more professional-looking finish.

Step 2: Use your cutting brush first to paint the edges and any door details. Only dip the top third of your cutting brush into the paint. This helps mitigate drips and gives you more control over where your paint goes.

Step 3: Immediately follow with your foam roller brush to cover the main surface area of the door. A foam roller brush is typically smaller than a regular roller brush, giving you more flexibility during painting. It's the best choice for doors because it hides brushstrokes!

Step 4: Repeat for a second coat, being sure to follow the drying instructions for your paint. A quality exterior paint should come with a sealer mixed in, so once your door is dry, it will last for quite some time.

Step 5: If you have a screen door, paint the trim the same color. Let everything dry completely before use.

DESIGN 101

DIFFICULTY LEVEL 1

DOOR HARDWARE UPGRADE

MATERIALS

- power drill w/ proper-size drill bits or handheld screwdriver
- hammer (optional)
- chisel (optional)
- new hardware (doorknobs and/or hinges)

Replacing a door's hardware, like its knob, may seem intimidating, but it is so easy! The quickest way to make the swap is to find newer hardware that is the same size as the old stuff. There should be a number stamped on it that gives you the doorknob's backset (the distance from the edge of the door to the center of the knob hole). This makes installation painless! Maybe you're in an older home, with outdated or generic locks and hinges. Often in rentals, you'll find them covered with paint from years of sloppy paint jobs. There should be super-cool hardware options available online or at your local hardware store. Going for a modern vibe? Try matte black hardware. Going vintage? Look for unlacquered brass.

Step 1: Remove old hardware with your power drill or handheld screwdriver, starting with the doorknob and ending with the lock. You may have to hammer a chisel into the old screws to chip any paint buildup off. (If you plan on painting the door, now's the perfect time! See opposite, "Painting Your Front Door," and wait for the paint to dry before moving on to the next step.)

Step 2: Now it's time to add the new stuff. Replace the doorknob first, lining up the inside knob with the existing hole in the door. Attach the exterior knob and secure it in place with the drill and package screws. Test it out and make sure the knob turns smoothly. Repeat with the dead-bolt lock.

Step 3: Go the extra mile and replace the hinges, too. Use a drill or screwdriver to replace one at a time, starting with the middle hinge. Unscrew the old screws on both the doorframe and the door, then discard the now-loosened hinge. Replace with the new hinge. Repeat for the top and bottom hinges, working on one at a time so that you don't have to take off the door completely as you work. Simple changes give an instant upgrade!

FLORAL EXPLOSION WELCOME MAT

MATERIALS

- computer printer
- X-Acto knife
- plain doormat
- painter's tape
- 8 stencil brushes
- outdoor acrylic paint (white, black, green, blue, red, orange, pink, and blue)
- floral stencil
- protective exterior paint sealer

Make your guests instantly feel welcomed into your home by creating a custom welcome mat that evokes the feeling of *Ahhh—it's so good to be here.* Why not add a pop of color that complements your door while you're at it? Feel free to add a larger black-and-white–striped outdoor rug under your Floral Explosion Welcome Mat for cool contrast.

Step 1: In boldface type and the largest size your printer can handle, print out each letter of the word *HELLO* on a separate piece of paper and cut out each letter using your X-Acto knife to create five stencils. Place them all onto the plain doormat, making sure they are centered, and secure with painter's tape.

Step 2: Dip a stencil brush into white paint, and dab off the excess. Less is more in this project to ensure precision—too much paint will bleed under the stencil. Paint over each letter until it's clearly legible on the doormat. Remove the stencil and let the paint dry.

Step 3: Prep the colorful paint and assign one brush to each color. Lay the floral stencil on the mat and begin to fill it in, starting at the edges, using the variety of colors in a somewhat random pattern. Use the same dabbing technique as in step 2. When you reach the *HELLO* in the middle, feel free to have some florals overlap letters or let it be.

Step 4: Let the paint dry completely. To finish, spray with a protective exterior paint sealer and let dry according to package instructions.

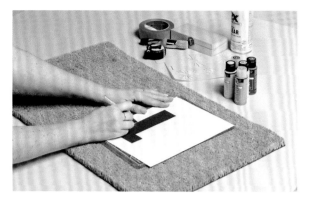

HOUSE NUMBER PLANTER BOX

MATERIALS

- pressure-treated wood
- 2 sawhorses
- handsaw or circular saw
- wood glue
- power drill
- non-rusting exterior wood screws
- sander
- 50- to 60-grit sandpaper
- landscape fabric
- wood stain (we used dark walnut)
- staining rag
- exterior paint sealer
- paintbrush
- metal house numbers
- rocks
- potting soil
- plants

House numbers are boring, but they don't have to be! This is an opportunity to incorporate the same metal as your new door hardware or mix in new materials. They can be hung vertically, horizontally, or asymmetrically—whatever works for your style. This house number planter box combo will take your front door up a notch!

Step 1: Measure and cut the wood by placing it on 2 sawhorses and using either a handsaw or a circular saw. Cut one piece to 4" × 24" for the back of the planter box and four pieces to 3½" × 3½" for the sides, front, and bottom.

Step 2: Assemble the planter box, starting with the sides. Dry-fit the wood pieces in the shape of the planter box (see "Life Hack: Dry-Fitting" on page 83 for an explanation of dry-fitting). Add a thin line of wood glue on all seams and press and hold for a few minutes.

Step 3: Mark ¼" in from all four corners on the front and back pieces and drill pilot holes. Then, drive in the exterior wood screws through the pilot holes to the adjoining boards. Place the base on top of the wood square (like a lid) and drill pilot holes ¼" in from all four corners of the base. Drive exterior wood screws down to attach the base. While the planter is still upside down, drill about three drainage holes (see "Life Hack: Making Drainage Holes" on page 27 to learn how).

Step 4: It's time to attach the planter to the main 4" × 24" wood piece. Squeeze a decent amount of wood glue on the back of the planter box and place onto the main wood piece 2" from the bottom. Let the glue dry for about 15 minutes. Drive in exterior wood screws from the back of the 4" × 24" piece into the planter box to secure the planter to the main wood.

Step 5: Lightly sand the entire piece using 50- to 60-grit sandpaper. If you are using cedar, it only needs a light sanding to buff out any rough edges. Cut a piece of the landscape fabric to fit inside the planter box, making sure to cut a few holes in the fabric to align with the drainage holes.

(continued)

Step 6: Stain the entire piece, using the exterior wood stain and a staining rag. After allowing it to dry, according to package instructions, apply a layer of exterior paint sealer with a paintbrush. Let it dry completely, according to package instructions, before moving on to the next step. Note: If you'd like to paint your planter, be sure to pick an exterior paint finish—these typically have sealer mixed in with the paint so no need to add a coat of sealer if you go this route!

Step 7: Attach the metal house numbers vertically using your drill. Mark out the spacing beforehand so the numbers are evenly spaced down the main wood piece.

Step 8: Now you're ready to plant! Drop a thin layer of rocks at the bottom of the planter, fill with potting soil, and plant your plants of choice (see our "Guide to Being a Good Plant Parent" on page 170). Water thoroughly.

Step 9: Use your drill to attach the planter to your house with one screw in each corner of the board. For brick houses, drive concrete anchors into the mortar. For wood or vinyl siding, use exterior wood screws. Stand back and admire your work!

WOOD PALLET STORAGE CATCH-ALL

MATERIALS

- French cleat
- wood pallet
- stud finder
- drill
- wood screws
- wall anchors
- wood shelf
- shelf brackets
- decorative hooks
- woven basket

This is a perfect way to add a mudroom to your entryway. We all need a place to toss our keys and hang our jackets—why not make it stylish? Don't let fancy terms like *French cleat* intimidate you (it's just a piece of hardware that enables you to hang things flush and securely on the wall!). This project is super easy and affordable to complete in an afternoon.

Step 1: Pick out a French cleat that fits in the center of your wood pallet. Use a stud finder to mark where the studs are located on your wall (see "Life Hack: Finding a Stud" opposite) and attach the wall side of the French cleat with a drill and wood screws, hitting those studs. Use wall anchors for screws that don't quite make it to a stud (see "Life Hack: Wall Anchors" on page 75 to learn how). Secure the other half of the French cleat to the back of the wood pallet with a drill and wood screws. Hang the pallet on the wall by sliding it on top of the wall-half of the French cleat.

Step 2: Attach a wood shelf about 16" from the bottom of the pallet. Use a drill and wood screws to secure the shelf brackets.

Step 3: Add a second shelf toward the upper right corner. At shoulder height, add 3 decorative hooks (perfect for dog leashes or extra grocery bags). Typically, these can be installed with a simple screw, but doublecheck the product instructions.

Step 4: Style out the shelves any way you'd like—consider adding a tray for your keys, a decorative crystal bowl to throw your mail in, and/or a small potted plant.

LIFE HACK: FINDING A STUD

Need help finding a stud? The best way to do so is to use a stud finder, available at any hardware store for under $20. Lay it flat, felt side against the wall. Follow package instructions to calibrate the tool, then slowly slide the stud finder horizontally across the wall. It will flash or beep when you've hit a stud—mark that spot with a pencil. Typically, studs are 16" apart. Go back and repeat your work on the same stretch of wall to double-check whether you've correctly marked the position of a stud.

CREATE A FOYER OASIS

MATERIALS

- 1 to 2 baskets
- bench, credenza, stool, or ottoman
- mirror, art print, or painting
- coat hooks or coatrack
- potted plant or vase with flowers

This four-step process is an easy-to-follow, foolproof way to set up an inviting entryway vignette. This applies to any size space, whether you have a grand foyer or minimal wall space by your front door (just adjust your furniture and décor to fit the scale, i.e., larger space = larger pieces). Pick a bench or a credenza. The benefit of a bench is that you have a place to put on shoes or boots before heading out the door. A credenza is great because it offers storage and a top surface to place a tray for keys and sunglasses. Choose whichever fits your lifestyle best. Note: For super-small spaces, go with an ottoman or stool.

Step 1: Place a basket (or two) to the right or left of your bench/credenza/stool/ottoman. You can't go wrong with a lovely woven basket to catch shoes or store umbrellas. Look for one that sits a few inches lower than your bench, stool, or ottoman or is half as tall as your credenza.

Step 2: Hang a mirror or a piece of art. Either choice will make a statement. A mirror is both practical (last looks before leaving!) and an optical illusion—light bounces off its reflective surface, making your entryway appear bigger. Large-scale art can fill the space in a dramatic way and immediately show off your personality and décor style. Art prints can lend a modern or quirky vibe with bold-lettered phrases. Paintings, especially those scored at flea markets, lend a vintage or traditional feel. If room, add coat hooks or a coatrack.

Step 3: Finish with a plant or a vase with flowers. Adding greenery to your home is always a good idea. An indoor tree, like a fiddle leaf fig, will make a beautiful vignette next to your bench. An interesting vase filled with flowers will be a refreshing greeting to your guests atop your credenza. If you have a small space, add a circular tray on top of your stool, then place a bowl for keys and a small bud vase filled with blooms on top of the tray, which can be easily moved if you need to use the stool. Voilà!

**LIFE HACK:
GO VERTICAL**
When decorating a
small space like an
entryway, decorate up
not out! Use vertical
space when available
to draw the eye
upward and make the
space appear bigger.

LIFE HACK: GO VERTICAL

Consider adding an automatic light timer to your entryway lamps so they switch on after the sun goes down. They are energy efficient, can help with time management, and add a sense of security to your home by signaling that it's occupied—great for when you're out of town for an extended period of time.

CREATE A PORTRAIT GALLERY WALL

MATERIALS

- framed photos
- kraft or butcher paper
- pencil
- scissors
- painter's tape
- hammer
- nails
- level
- museum putty

What better way to be greeted when you first enter your home than by the ones you love most? There are all kinds of gallery-wall layouts, and the good news is that there is no "right" way to do it. If you want a sleek, traditional vibe, use frames that are all the same size and color, hang them in a symmetrical grid, and consider using only black-and-white photos. Granny-eclectic-cottage style more your jam? Collect a mishmash of frames in different metals, sizes, and colors, and display a collection of vintage art prints in a sporadic pattern. Either way, use these tips to help create a gorgeous gallery wall for your entryway.

Step 1: Lay one of your framed photos on top of a large piece of kraft or butcher paper. Trace the outline of the frame with a pencil and cut out with scissors. On the paper cutout, mark where nails should go with the pencil. Also mark on the cutout which photo it refers to! Repeat with all the frames.

Step 2: Stick a piece of painter's tape on each paper cutout and begin to arrange them on the wall. It's easiest to start with the biggest frame and arrange the smaller ones around it. Rearrange the cutouts until you're happy with the spacing. Take a photo of each iteration to help you remember what you've already tried!

Step 3: Using your hammer, drive nails directly through the cutouts on the previously marked spots. Remove the cutouts from the wall and replace with the framed photos.

Step 4: Use a level to get each frame straight, then use museum putty to keep your frames in place (see "Life Hack: Museum Putty" at left).

Step 5: Snap a selfie with your new wall—you know you're gonna want to share your beautiful portrait gallery!

LIFE HACK: MUSEUM PUTTY

Museum putty is the best way to keep pictures straight on a wall! After you've hung up each frame, apply a small dot of putty to the back-bottom corners of the frame. Press firmly into the wall. Now your whole gallery will stay in place when inevitably bumped or jostled. By the way, museum putty is reusable, removable, and non-damaging!

page 60

page 50

Living Room

There is so much life lived in a living room (it's right there in the name). It's where roommates congregate after work, families have movie and game nights, and guests sometimes sleep. Upping your game in the room you spend so much of your time in can really improve your whole life.

A common problem: You live with a roommate or partner with a completely different style than you, resulting in a mishmash of furniture. Our 48-hour solution? Look for a project that can tie in both styles using similar colors and materials. For example, you like industrial style, but your roommate loves farmhouse chic. Dark metal or iron is a material that commonly shows up in both design aesthetics, so perhaps consider bringing in an armchair that has a cozy leather seat with metal armrests. Or choose artwork that depicts a landscape (hello, farmhouse), but is in black and white (hello, industrial). It's less about compromising your taste and more about finding pieces that reflect and complement both styles.

PICKING
THE RIGHT RUG

MATERIALS

- measuring tape
- painter's tape
- area rug
- rug pad

Not sure where to begin when decorating your living room? Start from the ground and work your way up! Having the right size rug will create the proper scale for a room, balance out the rest of the furniture, and make it feel cozier! Even with carpet, a layered-rug look is great. Here's how to make sure you pick the right rug.

Step 1: Let's assume you already have a sofa or sectional. Measure its length with your measuring tape. If your sofa is 84" long, add an additional 6" on each side to get the best width for your rug. So, in this scenario, you'd want an 8' × 10' rug.

Step 2: Use your painter's tape and measure out your "rug," putting tape on the floor in its shape. Move any existing furniture (like your sofa) into place on top of the taped-out rug. Double-check that at least the front legs of sofas and armchairs sit within the rug outline. You can even go bigger, with a 9' × 12' rug, if you'd like all legs of all seating to be on the rug.

Step 3: Splurge on the big rug. We promise, it will set your entire living room up for success! Make sure to add a rug pad, which will hold your rug in place and provide additional squishiness when you walk on top of it.

Step 4: If you own a rug you LOVE that is too small to fit the "legs of the furniture" rule, opt for a layered rug look. For example, pick out a jute rug that is the proper size as your base. Then layer the loved rug on top of the jute rug.

HANGING WINDOW TREATMENTS

MATERIALS

- measuring tape
- window treatment of your choice, including proper hanging hardware
- drill and screws
- wall anchors

The next step in setting up your living room is hanging window treatments! Curtains, Roman shades, or bamboo woven blinds are all great, but what's even better is when you layer more than one window treatment together. Just like adding a rug, picking and hanging a window treatment will immediately make your room feel cozy.

Step 1: Measure the width and length of your window, using your measuring tape. Additionally, grab the measurement from your ceiling to the floor. Many Roman shades or blinds hang with an inside mount, so be sure to measure the inside of your windowsill to get the proper measurement.

Step 2: Order the proper-size window treatment (see "Life Hack: Hanging Curtains" at left for curtain size advice). Make sure to get the right hanging hardware as well. For curtains, pick a rod that is at least 12" longer than the width of your window. For example, if your window is 72" long, get an extendable 44" to 108" rod. For Roman shades or bamboo woven blinds, use the hardware that comes with those window treatments.

Step 3: Use your drill and screws to hang up Roman shades or bamboo woven blinds on the top inside of your windowsill. For curtains, measure 4" out from the edge of your window, and the length of the curtain panel from the floor up (if your curtain is 90" long, measure 90" up from the floor). Install wall anchors (see "Life Hack: Wall Anchors" on page 75 to learn how) and secure the curtain rod in place with your drill and screws.

Step 4: Time to layer! Hang up woven shades for privacy, and then hang tall white curtains on top for a complete look. Plastic vertical blinds aren't exactly our top pick, but they often show up in rentals and starter homes because they are inexpensive and do the job just fine. If you can't uninstall them completely, try this trick: Pull the vertical shades to one side. Hang a *double* curtain rod and add sheer curtains to the back rod. These can stay closed all day and will act as your privacy shield while still letting in plenty of sunlight. Then, on the outer rod, hang decorative or blackout drapes that dovetail with your décor. Pull shut at night for total privacy.

LIFE HACK: HANGING CURTAINS

Hang your curtains as tall as possible to elongate the space and make your windows feel huge. Curtains falling 84" are almost always too short. As a general rule of thumb, look for curtains that are 90" and up. The hems should just kiss the floor for a clean look.

SUCCULENT COFFEE TABLE

MATERIALS

- drill
- simple wood storage box (coffee table–size)
- waterproof pond liner
- staple gun
- 4 round wooden furniture legs
- dry floral foam
- small rocks
- succulent soil
- a variety of succulents
- river rocks
- spray bottle
- 4 anti-slip pads for glass tabletops
- 2 towels
- ¼"-thick glass tabletop (you can order a custom-size piece of glass online)
- glass cleaner

If you're a plant lover and *into unique* furniture design, then this DIY is for you! Bring the outdoors in—this project is great for those who want to liven up their living room with greenery. A note before you start: If you're handy with a table saw and feel confident in building basics, you should feel empowered to construct the wooden coffee table base yourself—just skip the first step in these instructions!

Step 1: Using your drill, remove the top of your wood storage box by taking off the hinges. Discard the hinges and the top wood piece—you won't be needing them moving forward.

Step 2: Fully line the inside of the wood box with the waterproof pond liner, cut to size, and secure it in place with your staple gun. It should cover the bottom and the sides of the box, leaving about 2" of wood showing at the top.

Step 3: Attach the wooden furniture legs to each inside corner of the wood box by drilling them directly into the box's base. These will be the support for the glass top and will allow it to sit a little higher than the wood box for airflow, easy succulent access, and to prevent condensation.

Step 4: Now it's time to fill 'er up! Use large pieces of dry floral foam to fill the bottom half of the box. Next, add a layer of small rocks. Add plenty of succulent soil to completely cover the remainder of the base, filling it up with enough depth for your succulents to be planted. (For help choosing the right indoor succulents, check out page 176.) Now it's time to let your green thumb shine. Fill the entire surface area with succulents, adding a range of succulent varieties to lend visual interest and color variation. Cover any showing soil with pretty river rocks. Using a spray bottle, lightly spritz with water.

Step 5: Stick the anti-slip pads for glass tabletops on top of the wooden furniture legs. Use two towels to pick up the glass tabletop and place it on top of the wooden furniture legs (this will prevent fingerprint marks!). Clean off the top with glass cleaner. Keep styling simple and small—maybe a set of colorful coasters and a small rattan tray—you don't want

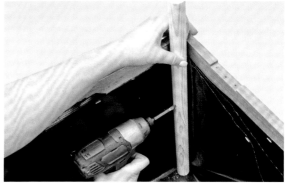

to obscure with your fabulous succulent masterpiece underneath the glass! Care for your plants as recommended, which, for succulents, means plenty of sunlight and only spritzing them with water when necessary, which is every time their soil dries out completely. The layers of dry floral foam and rocks at the bottom of the box will act as drainage—the good news about succulents is that they don't need a lot of water so you shouldn't be concerned about rot. Your succulent coffee table will be a showstopper in your living room and a lovely focal point.

DIFFICULTY LEVEL 1

DESIGN 101

DIY OMBRE TRIPTYCH

MATERIALS

- 3 rectangular canvas boards
- 12 (3-ounce) paper cups
- latex gloves
- 4 latex paint colors (we're using cream, magenta, pink, and blue in a satin finish)
- 3 (2") polyester paintbrushes
- 6" foam roller frame with 3 covers
- hammer
- 2" common nails
- level

LIFE HACK: PATCHING HOLES

Want to hang art on your walls but nervous about leaving a hole? Patching up nail holes is super easy—check out "REPAIRS 101: Teach Me How to Spackle" on page 225. Feel empowered to fill up your walls, knowing you can repair any holes later, and when you're ready to hang, firmly press a nail into the wall and give it a confident whack with a hammer.

The word triptych shows up a lot in design, and while it sounds super fancy, it's actually really simple! A triptych is a piece of artwork made up of three panels or pieces, typically hung side by side. You can stretch one image across all three panels, or just have complementary images styled together in a grouping. This project is the latter, with three ombre canvases.

Step 1: Place canvas number one on top of four 3-ounce paper cups, one in each corner (this elevation makes it easier to paint the sides!). Put your latex gloves on to protect your hands from the paint. Pour the cream paint directly onto the bottom of the canvas, and the magenta paint directly onto the top of the canvas. Using two paintbrushes, one for each color, make sweeping motions toward the center of the canvas to blend the two colors. Smooth out the paint to create an ombre effect, using a foam roller. Set aside the canvas to dry.

Step 2: Repeat with canvas number two, this time using the magenta at the bottom and the pink at the top. Blend the same way you did on the first canvas, using a new foam roller cover. Set aside to dry.

Step 3: Repeat with canvas number three, with pink at the bottom and blue at the top. Allow all the canvases to dry according to package instructions.

Step 4: Once dry, hang all three ombre canvases on an empty wall, using a hammer and 2" common nails. Use a level to make sure they are all straight (see "Life Hack: Museum Putty" on page 44). According to the traditional hanging method, triptychs should be hung in a row. But if you're feeling rebellious, you can hang them however you please (vertically, diagonally, or on opposite walls)—this is *your* space, and *you* get to decide what looks best. Step back and enjoy looking at your new masterpieces.

(continued)

MODERN DIPTYCH

MATERIALS

- 2 rectangular canvas boards
- painter's tape
- mixing bowl
- pencil
- clear all-purpose waterproof sealant
- paper towels
- 2 (2") polyester paintbrushes
- 2 latex paint colors in a satin finish
- hammer
- 2" common nails
- level

LIFE HACK: PAINTER'S TAPE

Painter's tape can help you work smarter, not harder. We have three hacks for you! (1) Remove tape before paint is fully dry to avoid peeling off dried paint. (2) To create irregular shapes, tear off smaller 1- to 2-inch pieces of painter's tape and overlap each piece by about ¼" to create a rounded edge. (3) Use clear all-purpose waterproof sealant on top of painter's tape to get a crisp line.

Given what you just learned about triptychs, we bet you can go ahead and guess what a diptych is. (Hint: It's two canvases instead of three.) A diptych is perfect for smaller spaces! This artwork makes a bold statement for any living room and should take less than an hour to create.

Step 1: Place the canvas boards facedown and tape together the seams, using your painter's tape. Add extra tape for support. Since this will be one continuous painted image stretched across both canvases, the tape will ensure they stay aligned during painting.

Step 2: Flip the canvases over and tape a triangle shape with painter's tape going over both panels. Let your artistic side come out to play here. Turn the mixing bowl over on one section of the canvas and trace the circle outline with your pencil. Tape off the outline of the circle with painter's tape (see "Life Hack: Painter's Tape" below).

Step 3: Apply the clear all-purpose waterproof sealant to the inside edges of the painter's tape, smoothing it out with your finger and wiping off the excess with a paper towel. This will prevent any paint from leaking under the tape and will give a crisp final product.

Step 4: Using two paintbrushes, one for each color, paint the various sections in the colors of your choice. Remove the painter's tape as soon as you're done, which now leaves you with two separate canvases. Let them dry completely according to package instructions.

Step 5: Using your hammer and 2" common nails, hang each canvas on the wall, either directly next to each other, or flanking two sides of a window. Use a level to make sure they are hung straight (plus use the museum putty hack on page 44).

 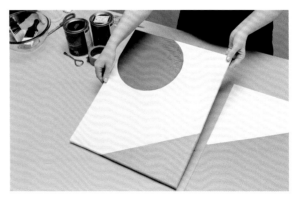

DIY PLANT PLANK WALL

MATERIALS

- 2 sawhorses
- 8 (1" × 4") wood boards (the length will depend on your wall—for example, if your wall is 84" long, cut wood boards to 60")
- sander or sanding block
- drop cloth
- vinyl gloves
- staining brush
- wood stain (we used dark walnut)
- plastic bowl
- stud finder
- painter's tape
- drill
- wood screws
- level
- hanging glass terrariums
- plant cuttings or air plants

If you envision yourself living in a plant-filled paradise, then this project is for you. It looks super custom and is a great way to fill vertical space on your walls. A plant plank wall wonderfully complements bohemian, midcentury modern, and Scandi-minimalist design aesthetics!

Step 1: Set up 2 sawhorses as your work surface. Place your wood boards on top and prep them by sanding all sides. This step is crucial because it gets rid of splinters and allows the stain to soak in properly. Wipe down each board with a drop cloth to remove any dust and debris.

Step 2: Put your vinyl gloves on to protect your hands from the wood stain. Using a staining brush, apply wood stain to 3 of the boards. Then pour around 1 cup of stain into a plastic bowl and dilute the stain with ½ cup of water to make a slightly lighter color. Then stain 3 more wood boards. Add another ½ cup of water to the stain and stain the remaining 2 wood boards.

Step 3: Using your stud finder (see "Life Hack: Finding a Stud" on page 37), mark locations of the studs on the wall with a piece of painter's tape. Put a separate piece on the floor as well to easily identify each stud location.

Step 4: Arrange the stained wood boards on the floor first to play around with your desired layout. Stagger them, arrange them to make different lengths—it's up to your artistic preference!

Step 5: Start attaching the wood boards to the wall by drilling screws through the pilot holes and into the studs. Use a level to make sure each board is straight.

(continued)

LIFE HACK: CUTTING WOOD
Need help cutting wood but don't own a saw? Most local hardware stores will do straight cuts for free! Try to go on a weekday to avoid weekend crowds (or just call first).

Step 6: Hang your glass terrariums from various points on the wood boards. Most glass terrariums hang from a simple hook nailed into the wood. It looks best when they are arranged randomly along the wall (rather than in a straight line). Plant cuttings work well in hanging glass terrariums—to learn how to grow plants from cuttings, check out page 185.

BRUSHED-YARN WALL HANGING

MATERIALS

- single-twist white cotton rope (81 pieces cut to 24")
- 6 skeins of colorful yarn (we're using 6 different colors here—you can use as many as you'd like!)
- scissors
- metal-bristled brush
- 36" wooden dowel
- hammer
- 2 flathead nails

This is an elevated and colorful take on the classic yarn hangings that have been circulating around social media. You can choose colors that complement your existing décor. Opt for bright colors to make a bold statement or, if you're going for a neutral look, pick shades of ivory and white.

Step 1: Fold 3 pieces of single-twist white cotton rope (each cut to 24") in half. Take one color of yarn and tie a knot 2" down from the top of the fold to tie the 3 cotton rope pieces together. There should be a small loop at the top.

Step 2: Begin wrapping the yarn down the length of the cotton rope, making sure that each loop around sits neatly underneath the one above it. Wrap about 6" to 8" down, tying a knot around the cotton rope. Use scissors to snip off the

end of the yarn, and repeat the process with each different color on new 3-piece white-rope combos.

Step 3: Use your metal-bristled brush on the ends of the cotton rope until they look soft and slightly frayed. Snip off the ends with your scissors to give it a clean line at the bottom.

Step 4: Slide each loop of your completed colorful rope pieces onto the wooden dowel until it's completely filled. (For reference, this took 81 pieces to fill up a 36" dowel.)

Step 5: Hammer 2 flathead nails into the wall, leaving three-fourths of the nail exposed. To install the finished piece, lay the dowel directly on top of those nails, with the brushed yarn hanging down.

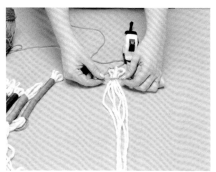

page
74

page
77

page
72

Kitchen

Have you ever walked into an older kitchen
and felt like you just walked into Grandma's? Besides a bathroom,
a kitchen is one of the first spaces in your home to feel dated. And
that's no fault of the builder or the original designer! Paint colors go
in and out of style, cabinet finishes evolve, and functionality shifts as
newer kitchen technology gets invented. That 1970s linoleum floor
and tile countertop were probably HOT STUFF when they were first
installed. It's tempting to want to smash everything like on TV demo
days, but there are actually many upgrades you can accomplish in
a 48-hour refresh that will instantly resolve this issue. Even adding a
vase of fresh flowers and giving the whole room a solid scrub down
can work wonders. But we bet you can do more. That you'll *want* to do
more. Get your moodboard ready, because having a kitchen you love
cooking in is totally worth it.

STENCILED FAUX-TILE BACKSPLASH

MATERIALS

- painter's tape
- stencil (either 6" × 6" or 8" × 8")
- level
- natural-bristle stencil brush or small foam roller
- satin-finish interior latex paint
- paper towel
- scissors

One of the most impactful ways to update your kitchen is to update the backsplash. For a super–budget-friendly option, consider stenciling a faux-tile pattern. If you have textured walls, use a natural-bristle stencil brush. This will help to prevent paint from bleeding underneath the stencil while you work. For smooth walls, a small foam roller will work great. If you're not sure what texture your walls are, go with a bristle stencil brush (it works for both!).

Step 1: Using painter's tape, tape off all surrounding walls and cabinets—basically anything that you *don't* want to get paint on. Then, tape your stencil up with a small piece of painter's tape, starting at the middle of the wall and working out. Use a level at the top of the stencil to ensure that the pattern is straight.

Step 2: Lightly dab the natural-bristle stencil brush in paint, and then tap it on a paper towel to get the excess off; otherwise the paint will bleed under the stencil and make your pattern look messy. Go slow and steady, filling in the stencil by dabbing the bristles perpendicular to the wall. Lift off the stencil; tape it to the next section of the wall, making sure to line up the pattern; and fill in the stencil again. Continue stenciling until your wall is covered.

Step 3: When you reach the corners and edges of the wall, you may need to cut your stencil to fit into a smaller space. That's okay! That's why you started in the middle. Let the paint dry according to package instructions.

PEEL-AND-STICK BACKSPLASH

MATERIALS

- degreaser
- paper towels
- peel-and-stick tile
- level
- screwdriver
- X-Acto knife

Another fabulous backsplash idea—this one temporary—is to use peel-and-stick tile. There are hundreds of options to choose from online. Before shelling out all your dough on the full amount of tile needed for your kitchen, purchase a sample piece. Not all walls are suitable for peel-and-stick (most manufacturers will list the types of walls that will support the stickiness of peel-and-stick!) You'll get to test it out on your wall to make sure it sticks *and* double-check that you like the color and pattern. Once you've picked out your peel-and-stick, and double-checked that it will work in your kitchen, you are ready to install— once you clean your walls, of course.

Step 1: Thoroughly clean your walls with a degreaser, like 409, and paper towels, and let it dry completely. Wipe down everything with a clean cloth to be extra sure it's dry. Your walls should be clean enough to pass a white-glove inspection.

Step 2: Starting from one side of the wall and working inward, peel a tile off its backing like a sticker and press it firmly to the wall for about 30 seconds. Use a level to make sure it's straight. Repeat this process with the next tile, making sure to line up the pattern. Keep working until the wall is covered.

Step 3: For areas on the wall that have an outlet, remove the outlet cover using a screwdriver. Hold the peel-and-stick tile against the wall, covering the outlet, and use the outlet cover to trace its location on top of the tile piece. Cut out the outlet shape with an X-Acto knife. Peel the tile off its backing and press onto the wall as with the others—your cutout hole should line up with the outlet! Reinstall the outlet cover over the peel-and-stick tile.

Step 4: Trim off any excess tile pieces with an X-Acto knife. If you see any gaps (because nearly all walls are not straight!) cut off extra pieces of tile and stick them to the wall. Later on, down the road when you're ready to change the peel-and-stick pattern, just peel the tiles off the wall. The magic of peel-and-stick!

CABINET HARDWARE UPGRADE

MATERIALS

- drill or screwdriver
- wood filler
- sander block
- new hardware
- adjustable punch-locator drill template
- screws

Beautiful new cabinet hardware is like the jewelry of your kitchen. Try matte black for a transitional style and antique bronze for a midcentury-modern style. Swapping out your hardware will instantly give your kitchen new life. It's quite uncommon for new hardware to perfectly line up with the drilled holes of the old hardware, so here's a guide on how to upgrade your cabinet accessories.

Step 1: Remove the old hardware with either a drill or a screwdriver (see "Life Hack: For Stripped Screws" opposite to help with pesky stripped screws). Fill in the old holes with wood filler. Let dry. Take your sander block and sand the wood filler down until it's smooth and flush with the rest of the cabinet. If you're painting your cabinets as well, check out "Cabinet Paint Upgrade" on page 84 for instructions!

Step 2: Adjustable punch-locator drill templates make it easy to know where to drill into your cabinets and drawer fronts (rather than individually measuring each time). Line up your new hardware on the adjustable punch-locator drill template and determine the correctly spaced holes to use. Line up the template on the cabinet front and drill new holes through the proper hole with your electric drill.

Step 3: Attach your pretty new hardware using the screws it came with and a drill or screwdriver. And, just like that, you've given your cabinets an instant face-lift!

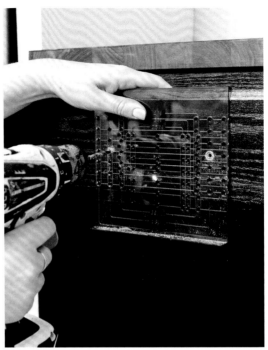

LIFE HACK: FOR STRIPPED SCREWS

If your kitchen is *really* old, there may be a stripped screw here or there. Not to worry—we have a trick to help you out. Take a rubber band and place it on the head of the screw. Press your electric drill on top and slowly reverse the screw out. The rubber band helps the drill "catch" despite the stripped edges of the screw.

ADDING SHELVING

MATERIALS

- stud finder
- drill
- screws
- wall anchors
- floating wood shelves
- level
- artwork, plants, and/or various plates, cups, or bowls

We love the idea of mixing traditional cabinets and open-concept shelving and this quick project is a great way to get a new look without a full-on kitchen renovation. First things first, find an open wall in your kitchen that has about 2 to 3 feet of wall space. Next, pull out and set aside all of your prettiest glassware, dishes, and kitchen tools, as well as a painting or a sculptural object or two. Now you're ready to get started.

Step 1: Check your wall for studs using your stud finder (see "Life Hack: Finding a Stud" on page 37 to learn how). Ideally, you want at least one half of the shelf to be screwed into a stud, since floating shelves need all the support they can get. Use your drill and screws to secure the wall anchors for the sides that don't hit a stud (see "Life Hack: Wall Anchors" opposite to learn how).

Step 2: Hang up your shelves with a level to make sure they are straight. For floating shelves, there is usually a metal anchor that comes with the shelf that gets attached to the wall with screws (and wall anchors), and then the shelf slides into it. Follow the instructions that come with your specific floating shelves. Leave about a foot vertically in between shelves. You can hang them staggered or directly lined up with one another.

Step 3: Fill your shelves with your pretty wares. Layer in a painting, leaned up against the wall, or plants atop a cake plate to add height variety, and play with stacking cups and bowls on top of each other. Don't feel like you have to fill the shelves to the brim. Leave a bit of white space and breathing room. Groupings of three are always a good idea if you're stuck on where to place items.

(continued)

LIFE HACK: WALL ANCHORS

Wall anchors are necessary when hanging anything that doesn't hit a stud. And they are quick to install! Using a drill, plus a drill bit the same size as the wall anchor, drill a hole into the designated spot on your wall. Push the anchor into the hole, using a hammer to lightly tap it into place. Switch your drill to a screw bit and drive a screw into the anchor. Now you're ready to hang!

MAGNETIC HERB GARDEN

MATERIALS

- 3 tins (cleaned and dried)
- super glue
- 3 gallon-size plastic baggies
- scissors
- floral foam
- potting soil
- herb plants (we love basil, rosemary, and thyme)
- 3 popsicle sticks
- black permanent marker
- heavy-duty magnets

Instead of a traditional window box, this project brings the garden inside so you can have your fresh herbs at your fingertips. Say goodbye to trips to the garden and rotten parsley in your crisper! If you're a big tea or coffee drinker, upcycle old metal tea or coffee tins for your herb garden. Or search for medium-size copper or galvanized-metal tins.

Step 1: Take one of your cleaned-out tins and apply super glue to the top rim. Quickly stuff a plastic baggie into the tin and press the top edges into the super glue to secure them in place. Let dry for a few minutes and then trim the excess plastic baggie, using your scissors. Repeat with the other tins.

Step 2: Place a few floral foam pieces at the bottom of one of the tins. This will help with drainage. Sprinkle a bit of potting soil into the tin and then add one herb plant. Be sure to loosen the roots before planting. Top off with more potting soil as needed, pressing down gently with your fingers to secure the herb into the container. Repeat with the rest of the tins. Lightly water all three tins.

Step 3: Now it's time to make your plant markers. Take a popsicle stick and turn it sideways. Using a black permanent marker, neatly write out the name of the herb. Let the words fully dry before sticking the bottom half of the popsicle stick into the herb tin.

Step 4: Pop a heavy-duty magnet onto the back of each tin. Depending on the type of metal your tins are made of, the magnets might stick to them. But if they don't, or if they aren't sticking securely, put a dab of super glue on the back of each magnet and press them firmly onto the metal tins. Stick your new herb garden magnets to your fridge and get cooking!

LIFE HACK:
Keep your herbs fresh by caring for them correctly! Water when the top layer of soil is dry. Allow them to sit in the sun at least once per week.

WALL-MOUNTED FOLDING TABLE

MATERIALS

- 2 pieces of 20" × 2" wood
- 1 piece of 20" × 30" wood
- 1 piece of 20" × 36" wood
- sander
- 2 (18") heavy-duty piano cabinet hinges
- drill
- wood screws
- 2 non-skid rubber bumpers
- stud finder
- measuring tape
- pencil
- level
- 1 casement fastener
- painter's tape
- caulk
- roller brush
- black chalkboard paint
- wood oil conditioner
- clean cloth
- chalk

This serious space-saving hack is perfect for a small apartment or a mini–breakfast nook. It's like a Murphy bed concept in kitchen-table form. Plus, you can get creative with your chalk art on the front of the table—perhaps write out your weekly menu, a morning greeting to start your day with a smile, or ingredients for a favorite recipe! We'd classify this as more of an advanced DIY project, but it can still be completed within a weekend.

Step 1: Make sure all the wood is cut to size (see "Life Hack: Cutting Wood" on page 61 if you need help cutting your wood). Sand down all wood pieces to get rid of pesky splinters. An electric sander is going to be ideal here and make this step go much faster. The 20" × 36" piece will be the top of the table. The 20" × 30" piece will be the side. The 20" × 2" pieces will be the wall-mounted pieces.

Step 2: Lay the top and side pieces perpendicular to each other and attach one of the piano cabinet hinges using your drill and wood screws. There should be about a 1" lip over the top of the side piece.

Step 3: Drill a pilot hole in each of the bottom two corners of each side piece. Screw in the rubber bumpers by hand.

Step 4: Use your stud finder and mark the studs on the wall (see "Life Hack: Finding a Stud" on page 37). This is going to be a heavy piece of furniture, so you *must* screw the wood into studs to ensure that the table is secure. Additionally, measure and make a pencil mark on the wall 30" from the floor—this is how tall your table will be. Take one of the wall-mounted pieces of wood and screw it into the wall at the 30" mark. There should be a screw at 2" and 18" on the wall-mounted wood. Use your level to make sure it's straight.

Step 5: Dry-fit the table on top of the wall-mounted wood (see "Life Hack: Dry-Fitting" on page 83 for an explanation of dry-fitting). Mark where the piano cabinet hinge fits (about 1" in from each edge) and attach it with a drill and screws to both the tabletop and the wall-mounted sides. Now the table part is done.

(continued)

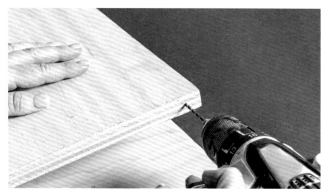

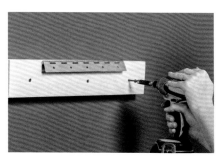

Step 8: Your table is fully functioning and foldable now, so let's take it up a notch with chalkboard paint! Using your painter's tape, mark an 18" × 28" rectangle on the front of the side piece (see "Life Hack: Caulk Trick" on page 85 to learn how to use caulk to get a super-even paint line).

Step 9: Load up your roller brush with black chalkboard paint and fill in the rectangle completely. You'll probably need to do two coats. Peel off the tape once that second coat is done and let the paint dry for a solid 2 hours.

Step 10: Finish off the rest of the table with wood oil conditioner. Squeeze a blob of conditioner onto a clean cloth and spread evenly over all the unpainted wood. Let it sit for about 5 minutes and then wipe off any excess.

Step 11: Using your chalk, write out something fun on the chalkboard!

Step 6: Now it's time to mark where the top wall-mounted wood piece should go. Again, find the wood studs and screw directly into those at the 2" and 18" marks on your wood piece. Use your level to make it straight.

Step 7: Measure and mark the center point for the table and the top wall-mounted wood piece. Using your drill and screws, attach the casement fastener at that center point to both the top wall-mounted wood piece and the underside of the lip of the tabletop.

CABINET PAINT UPGRADE

MATERIALS

- drill
- small plastic baggies
- degreasing wet wipes
- paper towels
- electric sander
- 100- to 150-grit sandpaper
- rag
- spray shelter
- paint sprayer
- semigloss latex paint
- 3-ounce paper cups
- painter's tape
- paint tray
- 2-inch shortcut polyester angle sash cutting brush
- 6-inch foam roller
- polycrylic protective finish
- vinyl gloves (optional)

Painting old cabinets a fresh color will make a major impact in your kitchen. By following these steps, you'll get a professional-looking paint job without breaking the bank. Consider painting your uppers and lowers different colors for a multidimensional modern look. The key to making them look brand-new is to Take. Your. Time. This is a 101 that will probably take the full 48 hours of your weekend.

Step 1: Remove cabinet doors one at a time, using a drill to unscrew old hardware. Make sure to label each door so you know which cabinet it belongs to, and store the hinges and screws for each door in their own small plastic baggie so they don't get mixed up with the hardware from the other doors. Label the baggies as well and store in a safe spot.

Step 2: Wipe down all surfaces with degreaser wet wipes. Follow with paper towels to make sure everything is dry.

Step 3: Using your electric sander and 100- to 150-grit sandpaper, thoroughly sand all sides of the cabinet doors and the cabinet boxes inside the kitchen. This will knock off old paint, ensure a smooth finish, and help the new paint stick to the cabinet surfaces. Clean up all dust with a wet rag, followed by a dry paper towel.

Step 4: Set up the spray shelter in an outside area (yards, garages, or even balconies can work)—it should look like a three-sided tent. Get your paint sprayer loaded up with paint. Follow the sprayer's instructions to make sure you have the proper amount of paint inside. You can certainly choose to hand-paint each cabinet door, but a sprayer will cut your painting time in half and give a super-smooth finish. Spray all fronts of the cabinet doors with new paint, making sure not to spray too closely (this can cause drips). Set cabinet doors aside to dry on top of 3-ounce paper cups to keep them lifted off the ground. Once dry, repeat for the backs of the cabinets.

Step 5: While waiting for the cabinet doors to dry, head back inside to paint the cabinet box. First, use painter's tape to tape off any surfaces you don't want paint on. Next, pour some of the paint into a paint tray. Then use your cutting brush to get paint into all the nooks and crannies. Use a foam roller on bigger areas and to cover up any potential streaks from your cutting brush. Immediately remove the tape when you're done painting.

Step 6: After the cabinets are completely dry (we recommend waiting at least 24 hours), use a foam roller or a cleaned-out paint sprayer to apply a layer of polycrylic protective finish to both the cabinet doors and the cabinet boxes. Kitchens are a high-traffic area, so you want to be sure your new cabinets are protected.

Step 7: After the proper drying time (double-check the package instructions), you can either add new cabinet hardware (see page 72) or reattach the old hardware—both options require a drill. Now your cabinet doors are ready to be reinstalled. Because you labeled each door with its location, it should be easy to reassemble your kitchen. (If you went with a light paint color, it's a good idea to wear vinyl gloves so you don't get fingerprints on your new cabinets.)

LIFE HACK: CAULK TRICK

One of the best ways to ensure a super-straight paint line is to use the painter's tape + white paintable latex caulk trick. After affixing your painter's tape, squeeze a thin line of caulk along the edge. Wipe down the caulk line using your finger and a paper towel so the line is flat and smooth over the tape. After you're done painting, remove the painter's tape—the caulk acts as a sealer to prevent paint seepage under the tape!

page 88

page 92

page 96

page 165

Bed**room**

There are books out there that will tell you that you spend most of your life in your bedroom . . . or maybe it's sleeping . . . or both? Who cares! It doesn't matter how much time you spend there—when you walk in, you want an intimate, cozy sanctuary and an inviting space to rest and relax. Your bedroom should be an oasis that reflects your passions and your comforts.

If you're finding that you aren't getting a good night's sleep, it could be your décor that's the issue. Color theory, which is the way colors affect our moods and make us feel, is important in all spaces, but especially in your bedroom. Blues, whites, and greens are all colors that offer serenity to our subconscious. Try to find ways to incorporate brighter colors that you love in artwork or a pillow pattern while letting those calming colors take the main stage.

Oftentimes, the "public" spaces in our homes become the first priority when refreshing and we totally get it—they are more on display when guests come to visit, and we all want to feel comfortable hosting in "finished" rooms in our homes. But, remember: Your bedroom is just as important. When you have a place to retreat to at the end of a long day, where you can recharge, rest, and relax, you are much more likely to feel refreshed each morning.

OMBRE CURTAINS

MATERIALS

- plastic drop cloth or worktable
- Rit fabric dye (we're using tangerine and golden yellow)
- mixing bottle (a 24-ounce plastic water bottle works great)
- gallon-size plastic bin
- plain white curtains
- rubber gloves
- kosher salt
- spray bottle

Elevate plain white curtains with this fun DIY project. Pick a complementary or accent color and get ready to make your curtains command attention. Simple linen curtains are best to really let the ombre color shine. Blackout-lined panels may be too heavy for the dye to soak through, and sheers won't absorb the color enough. See "Bedroom Setup Basics" on page 91 for advice when hanging bedroom window treatments!

Step 1: Gather your materials and get set up in an outdoor area like your yard, garage, or balcony. Lay out a plastic drop cloth or set up a worktable you don't mind getting messy. You don't want to worry about dye splashing and staining anything but the curtains!

Step 2: Combine the dyes in the mixing bottle to create the perfect color. (Remember to put on your rubber gloves first . . . unless you want your hands dyed,

too!) There is no exact formula here; it's mostly based on personal preference. But start with 4 ounces of golden yellow and add 2 ounces of tangerine to achieve a rich orange-yellow ombre. Shake the mixing bottle to combine the colors.

Step 3: Fill your gallon-size plastic bin with water heated to 140°F. The bin should be about three-fourths of the way filled.

Step 4: Dunk the white curtains in the water, getting them completely wet. This will allow the curtains to completely absorb the dye later on. Wring them out to remove all excess water. Lay the curtains next to the water bin, leaving the bottom half of the fabric sitting in the water. Even though just the bottom half will be dyed, it's a good idea to get the whole curtain wet to allow a natural-looking spread throughout the fabric.

Step 5: Time to add the dye! Pour a generous amount of dye (about half of your dye water bottle) into the water bin and mix it into the water. Add about ½ cup of kosher salt to activate the dye. Thoroughly mix the dye and the salt together.

(continued)

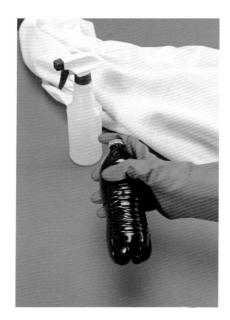
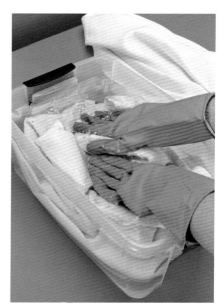
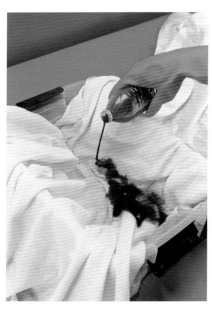

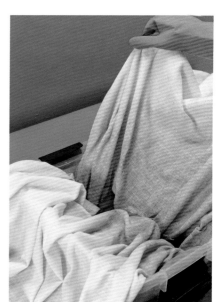

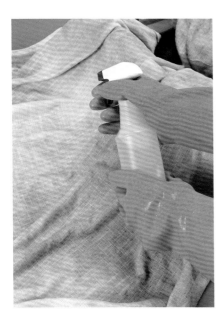

Step 6: Slowly pull the drapes out of the dye bath a couple of inches at a time every 6 minutes. The longer the fabric is submerged, the deeper the hue. Add the remainder of the bottle of dye to the bath to make the bottom edge of the curtain panel a rich color.

Step 7: Use a spray bottle filled with water to spritz the fabric that's already been pulled out of the bin. This blends the ombre even further. Continue doing this until you get to the bottom edge of the curtains. Wring out excess water once the entire curtain has been completed.

Step 8: Hang and let air-dry completely before ironing and hanging up in your bedroom.

BEDROOM SETUP BASICS

Here are the basics when setting up your bedroom with functionality in mind: How much space you have will determine what exactly you can include in your design. For teeny-tiny bedrooms, focus on a fabulous bed with at least one nightstand and a side light standing on it. You can even install a plug-in sconce mounted on the wall above the nightstand to free up tabletop space. From there, square footage permitting, consider adding bench seating at the foot of your bed and a cozy accent chair in the corner with a small side table. Having multiple seating areas will enable you to use your bedroom as more than just a place to sleep.

No matter what the size of your space, consider some sort of window treatment, which is key to cultivating a calming bedroom space. Consider your sleep patterns. If you need total darkness to catch some zzz's, opt for blackout curtains layered over sheers that will allow light to filter in during the day. If you like to wake up with the sunrise, look into Roman shades made out of lighter fabric—you'll get privacy at night but pretty rays in the morning. An area rug is always a good idea to ramp up the homey factor. Be sure to pick a large-size rug that extends at least 24" on either side of your bed. Layer on a fluffy sheepskin rug for maximum comfort.

CHANNEL-TUFTED HEADBOARD

MATERIALS

- 3 (1" × 12") wood boards *
- 3 pieces of upholstery foam (cut to the size of the wood boards)
- spray adhesive (Gorilla Glue spray adhesive is super durable)
- velvet fabric
- batting
- staple gun
- 2 metal strap ties
- drill
- wood screws
- measuring tape
- French cleat
- level
- pencil
- wall anchors

*3 (1" × 12") wood boards (length depends on the size of your bed):
- twin bed = 40"
- full bed = 53"
- queen bed = 62"
- king bed = 78"

Get ready to make a statement with this bold project! Why spend hundreds of dollars on a store-bought headboard when you can make a customized one for your bedroom instead? Shockingly, velvet is very durable, despite looking delicate. Plus, the height of this headboard will provide the perfect focal point for your room, helping to make it comfortable and stylish at the same time.

Step 1: This project can be done right on the floor of your bedroom—just remember to sweep before getting started. Lay out the 3 wood boards next to the 3 pieces of upholstery foam. Spritz the spray adhesive onto the top of a wood board and stick a foam piece onto it, pressing firmly. Repeat with the other 2 boards. Let dry for about 15 minutes.

Step 2: Lay out your velvet fabric on the floor. Lay the batting right on top. Cut both to the size of one of the wood/foam pieces, leaving 6" of excess on each side, and repeat with the other three pieces. For a twin bed, make each fabric/batting piece 24" × 52"; for a full bed, make each fabric/batting piece 24" × 65"; for a queen bed, make each fabric/batting piece 24" × 74"; for a king bed, make each fabric/batting piece 24" × 90". Set the fabric aside.

Step 3: Place a wood/foam piece on top of a cut batting piece with the foam side facing down toward the batting. Stretch the batting layer up and over the foam toward the back side of the wood, and staple it in place, using your staple gun. Alternate left and right sides for each staple so that the batting is evenly stretched. Do the corners last. Fold the corners up and in (like wrapping a present!) to make a rounded edge on all four corners. Repeat with the fabric, using the same alternating technique. Repeat step 3 with the other 2 wood boards.

Step 4: Line up the upholstered boards on the floor, fabric side down, to form the headboard. For a twin bed, the headboard

(continued)

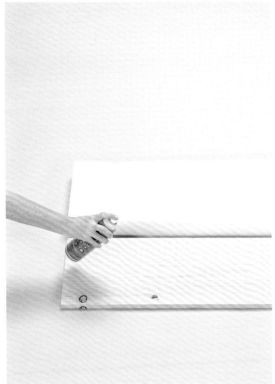
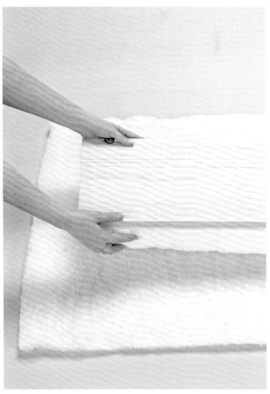

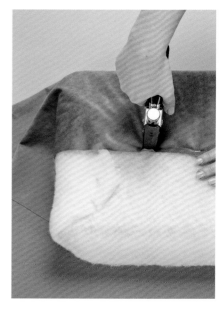

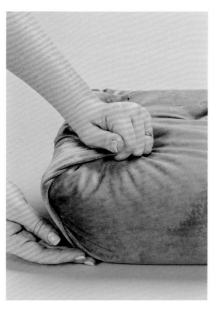

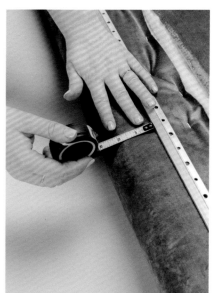

should be 36" tall × 40" long; for a full bed, the headboard should be 36" tall × 53" long; for a queen bed, the headboard should be 36" tall × 62" long; for a king bed, the headboard should be 36" tall × 78" long. Attach the boards together with 2 metal strap ties, 1 on the far left side, and the other on the far right side. Secure the strap ties to the wood boards, using your drill and wood screws. Now all 3 boards should be securely attached to one another.

Step 5: Time to get your headboard ready to mount on the wall. Use a measuring tape to find the center of the top wood board, and screw in the French cleat there. It's always a good idea to use a level to ensure a straight line both on the headboard and on the wall. Use your measuring tape to mark the center point of your bed and position the adjoining cleat onto the wall. FYI: Your headboard should line up with the top of your mattress. Mark where each screw will go with a pencil, drill pilot holes, and then hammer in wall anchors. (See "Life Hack: Wall Anchors" on page 75 to learn how to correctly install a wall anchor.)

Step 6: Attach the rest of the French cleat by drilling screws into the wall anchors, and hang up your new headboard.

REFINISHED FLUTED NIGHTSTANDS

MATERIALS

- nightstand
- sander
- cloth
- chalked spray paint
- latex gloves
- wood pole wrap
- table saw or handheld hacksaw
- measuring tape
- wood glue
- edge pull (optional)
- drill (optional)

Is there anything more satisfying than flipping a piece of furniture? Not only is it a sustainable method of decorating, but it's also a lot of fun to do. Take your tired old nightstand, give it a little love, and you've got a completely redesigned space. If you don't already own a piece of furniture to flip, check out a local secondhand furniture store, visit a thrift shop, or look online! The main criteria are that it has at least one functioning drawer and that it's the proper height in relation to your bed (24" to 27" is the ideal nightstand height). Look past the scratches, ugly stain or color, and dated hardware—all of that can be changed.

Step 1: Scuff-sand all surfaces of the nightstand (check out "Life Hack: Scuff-sanding" opposite to learn how to scuff-sand). It doesn't have be sanded down to the original wood; rather, knock off any sheen or topcoat finish. Buff out scratches, too. Wipe off any sawdust with a damp cloth.

Step 2: Spray all surfaces with chalked spray paint. One of the biggest benefits of chalk paint is that it adheres to most surfaces really easily. And by using a spray-paint version, you'll get a smoother finish. Just be sure to do 2 or 3 light layers, sprayed from 6" away. If you get too close when you spray-paint, you run the risk of paint drips. Wear latex gloves to help keep the paint off your hands.

Step 3: While the paint is drying, it's time to cut the wood pole wrap with a table saw or a handheld saw for the front of the drawer. For a drawer front that is 10" tall, cut the wood pole wrap at 9¾".

Step 4: Lay the nightstand flat with the drawer front facing up. Spread a thin layer of wood glue onto the back of the pole wrap and attach it to the drawer front. Let dry for 1 hour.

Step 5: Slide the nightstand into place next to your bed. Optionally, attach an edge pull to the drawer front, using the screws that come with it and a drill. Style out your new nightstand.

LIFE HACK: SCUFF-SANDING

Scuff-sanding takes off the top layer of existing stain or finish and works best for repainting furniture. It's perfect for projects like flipping furniture because it knocks off the exiting sheen and gets your furniture ready for refinishing.

LIFE HACK: MIRRORS

Adding mirrors to your space, whether it's on a wardrobe or a wall, reflects natural light and gives the illusion of a bigger and brighter space. Bring on the mirrors!

CUSTOM WARDROBE UPGRADE

MATERIALS

- wardrobe
- drill
- grass cloth peel-and-stick wallpaper
- smoother tool
- X-Acto knife
- measuring tape
- pencil
- 2 full-body mirrors
- black handles
- painter's tape
- level
- screws
- coat hooks (we like to use individual oversized acrylic pegs)

No closet? No problem! Take your existing, plain wardrobe up a couple notches with this simple upgrade. This is perfect for a dorm room or a bedroom without a built-in closet. By jazzing up the façade of your wardrobe, you'll want to keep it as a permanent solution and staple of your bedroom.

Step 1: Remove existing wardrobe handles by using your drill to unscrew all screws. Toss these old screws aside—you won't be needing them moving forward!

Step 2: Starting at the top of one of the wardrobe doors, hang up the grass cloth peel-and-stick wallpaper by peeling back a little at the top, sticking it to the door front, and smoothing it down toward the bottom of the door with your smoother tool. It's like installing a big sticker. Cut off excess wallpaper with your X-Acto knife, trimming off any wallpaper sticking out over the edges of the door. Repeat with the other door front.

Step 3: Measure and mark with a pencil the center point for where the mirrors will hang—one on each door. Drill the necessary holes, and hang up the mirrors with the hardware they came with.

Step 4: Next up is attaching the new black handles. To get the top and bottom handle holes perfectly aligned, place a piece of painter's tape on the back of the handle and poke two holes where the screws need to go. Then peel off the tape and stick it to the door in the desired location (usually at waist height), using a level to ensure straight lines. Use your drill to drive screws right into the spots marked on the tape. Peel off the tape and attach the handles.

Step 5: Move to the side of the wardrobe to install the coat hooks. If you're using individual oversized acrylic pegs, they can be installed by drilling a screw into the wardrobe and then twisting the peg onto the screw.

Step 6: Hang bags or hats on the acrylic pegs. Your wardrobe has officially been customized and upgraded in less than an afternoon.

DESIGN 101

ROSEMARY-LAVENDER SACHET

MATERIALS

- fresh rosemary
- fresh lavender
- mortar and pestle
- drawstring linen sachet
- lavender essential oil
- ribbon or twine

Keep your closet smelling fresh with this homemade deodorizer. Lavender is a homeopathic remedy for sleep support, and rosemary is linked to improving mood and relieving stress. So this sachet will make your clothes smell good and make you feel great. Bonus: These also make great gifts!

Step 1: Strip the rosemary leaves and lavender flowers from their stems and combine in the mortar. Lightly grind with the pestle to release their natural fragrances. Empty into the linen sachet until it's full.

Step 2: Add a few drops of the lavender essential oil and pull the drawstring of the sachet closed. Shake to combine the essential oil with the rosemary and lavender.

Step 3: Add a little extra flair by tying a small piece of ribbon or twine around the top of the sachet. Place in your closet, wardrobe, or dresser drawer. Replace once you notice that the scent has faded.

page
106

Multipurpose Room

We've all got that one room in our house that we have to use for EVERYTHING.

The problem? Your multipurpose room feels like a total, jumbled mess. The best solution here is twofold: One, allocate designated "zones" to delineate between functions, and two, use a cohesive color palette throughout the space. Let's talk through a guest room–office as an example. Take one corner of the room and dub it your office space. Find a desk with storage to contain all the office "things" in one space. Painted shapes on walls serve as a great, inexpensive way to add architectural interest and offer visual separation between the spaces.

The other half of the room is now designated as a guest room. Choose textiles that pick up the colors of the painted feature wall to tie both sides together. When you have guests staying with you, make a point to tidy up your workspace and consider adding a "Go the Extra Mile" Guest Basket (page 165) at the foot of the guest bed.

Look at you—entertaining *and* killing it at work. An intentionally designed space can promote success in both arenas. Read on for more 101s to make the most out of those multipurpose spaces.

FUNCTIONAL ROOM DIVIDER

MATERIALS

- large white bookcase (with cubbies)
- sheets of lauan (to fit the back of the bookshelf)
- circular saw
- staple gun + staples
- peel-and-stick wallpaper
- smoother tool
- X-Acto knife
- French cleat (optional)
- books, pictures, and wicker baskets

A basic bookcase can double as a room divider. Pick up an average-looking, white-cubed bookcase and make it look like a million bucks with this DIY trick. You'll be able to increase the uses of your space simply by sectioning it off without compromising on storage or design.

Step 1: Assemble the white bookshelf, cubbies and all. If you got it from a store like IKEA, then this may take a while, but be sure to follow all assembly instructions. Leave the bookshelf lying on the floor for the next step.

Step 2: Cut lauan to fit the back of the bookshelf, using a circular saw. Attach to the bookshelf, using your pneumatic stapler. Add a staple every 6", going all the way around the border. Leave the top row of cubbies exposed—this is mostly for decorative purposes, but it also allows light to stream through on both sides of the divider.

Step 3: Have a friend help you stand your bookcase upright and begin to attach the peel-and-stick wallpaper to the back on top of the attached lauan. Smooth out bumps or creases with your smoother tool and use your X-Acto knife to cut off any excess around the edges.

Step 4: Move your bookcase into position—now it's officially a room divider! One side—bedroom; the other side—office. For extra security, attach it to the wall by screwing in a French cleat (often included with the bookcase).

Step 5: Decorate the cubbies with books and pictures, and use wicker baskets for more storage opportunities. Voilà—two rooms in one!

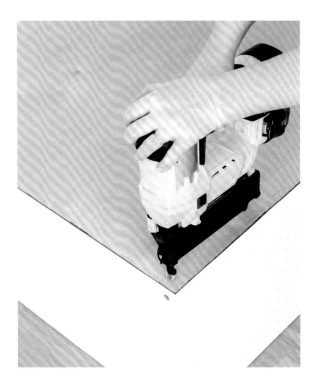

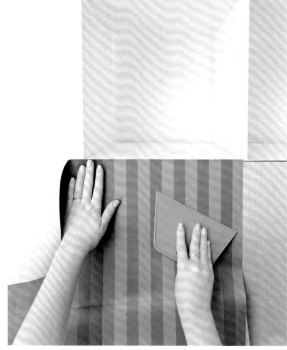

LIFE HACK: INSTALLING REMOVABLE WALLPAPER

Here's a guide to installing removable wallpaper: To hang, first measure out the width of the wallpaper strip from the left side of the wall. Make a mark with a pencil, and then use a level to lightly draw a straight line down the length of the wall. This will be your guide to hanging the wallpaper straight, rather than using the wall because, for whatever reason, most walls aren't perfectly straight! Peel off a section of wallpaper and begin hanging from the top of the wall like a sticker, using your smoother tool to get out any bumps and lumps. Once you reach the bottom of the wall, use an X-Acto knife to cut off any extra wallpaper. Repeat by lining up the next panel with the pattern repeat on the panel you've already installed. Keep going until the wall is covered.

BUILT-IN DESK

MATERIALS

- spackle
- cloth
- removable wallpaper or paint
- filing cabinet (16" l × 21" d × 22" t)
- measuring tape
- pencil
- stud finder
- drill
- wood screws
- wood board (21" l × 4" d × 2" t)
- level
- desktop (butcher block is great; 48" l × 30" d × 1½" t)
- plug-in wall sconce (optional)
- shelves (optional)
- desk chair

For those of us without a designated home office room, this is a great way to still get a home office *space*. Maybe you have a nook under the stairs that you have no idea what to do with. Or you have an underutilized closet that could be a perfect spot for a desk, as long as you take off the closet doors and get a little creative. This project is a great way to use every inch of your space and makes working from home so much easier.

Step 1: Remove anything currently in the space, patch up holes with spackle (see "REPAIRS 101: Teach Me How to Spackle" on page 225 to learn how to spackle properly), and do a full wipe-down with a damp cloth to get rid of dust, dirt, and debris.

Step 2: Hang up the removable wallpaper (see "Life Hack: Installing Removable Wallpaper" on page 105) or paint a shape onto the wall above the desk. This is a great opportunity for a color and pattern moment or to keep it neutral and serene with a softer design.

Step 3: Slide your filing cabinet into place on one end of the designated space. Measure and mark with a pencil the same height as the filing cabinet on the opposite wall. Use your stud finder to mark where the studs are (see "Life Hack: Finding a Stud" on page 37), and use your drill and wood screws to secure the 21" × 4" × 2" wood piece horizontally into those studs. Use a level to make sure it's straight.

Step 4: Set your desktop on top of the filing cabinet and horizontal wood side support from step 3. It should be level because of your accurate measuring skills. For extra security, drive a screw, using your drill, from the top of the desktop down into the wood side support. Be sure to drill a pilot hole first!

(continued)

Step 5: If space permits, install a plug-in wall sconce 18″ above the wood side support, using your drill. A sconce (rather than a table lamp) is a great hack for freeing up desk space when you're working with a smaller area. Double-check that you're using a plug-in sconce, rather than a hardwired sconce. You'll know it's a plug-in because it, well, plugs into an outlet.

Step 6: If space permits, install 1 or 2 shelves above the desk, using your drill, a level, and the proper screws. Make sure you place them high enough to leave space for your computer monitor.

Step 7: Add personal décor touches, slide in your desk chair, and you are ready to get to work. Since your new home office is in a multiuse area, keep your desk tidy by utilizing baskets for paperwork and jars or cups for pens.

TOP 5 FURNITURE PIECES
FOR A MULTIUSE SPACE

Adding multifunctional furniture to any room doubles and sometimes triples your space. A futon folds out to become a bed. The top of your ottoman is removable and reveals storage underneath. Here are our top five suggestions to make the most out of your room.

DAYBED

This is perfect for a home office/guest room combo because it takes up way less space than a traditional bed and serves as a comfortable lounge sofa during the day. You'll feel more like you're at the office while working from home if you aren't in the middle of a bedroom. Style out the daybed with lots of pillows, mixing color and texture for a layered look. And when your parents are in town? Store those decorative pillows away and make up the bed with sheets and blankets.

STORAGE OTTOMANS

These are perfect for most combination rooms. Have a guest room/office space? Store office supplies or extra blankets. Using your room as a dining room/schoolhouse? A storage ottoman can serve as extra seating in either scenario and store seasonal dishware or backup school supplies.

LADDER DESK

If you need a workspace but you've run *out* of space, think vertically. A ladder desk is the best option for a small studio apartment, or a craft closet, because it takes up vertical space, rather than valuable floor-space real estate. Most come with one or two shelves up above, so make use of that space to hold baskets and books.

STORAGE LADDER

This simple piece of furniture doubles as storage and décor. By leaning it against the wall in your bedroom or living room, you have a space to display your prettiest throw blankets or quilts. Use it in your bathroom over the toilet area for towels and storage of various toiletries.

C-SHAPED SIDE TABLE

Also known as a "laptop table," this is great for those who want to have the function of a desktop but don't necessarily have the space for it. Simply slide it up to your sofa or armchair and get working. Bonus: It can act as a makeshift dining table. Perfect for holding drinks and snacks for your next movie night.

TRUNDLE DOG BED

MATERIALS

- 4 wood boards for siding*
- piece of plywood**
- table saw or handheld hacksaw
- sanding block or small electric sander
- cloth
- wood glue
- drill
- 1½" wood screws
- 4 swivel locking casters
- pencil
- vinyl gloves
- wood stain (we used dark walnut)
- staining rag
- dog bed cushion
- dog

We love our furry friends here at Tastemade, and what better way to show how much you care than by making them a custom bed? This is perfect for those multiuse spaces because when your dog isn't using it, the trundle rolls right under your bed or couch.

Step 1: Cut the 4 wood boards to size for the siding pieces, as well as the plywood, using a table saw or a handheld hacksaw (see sizing guide below to get the proper measurements). Sand all the wood pieces—you can use a sanding block, but for ease, try out a small electric sander. Use a damp cloth to wipe off residual dust.

Step 2: Assemble all the pieces to form the bed. Apply a thin line of wood glue along the edges of the plywood base and firmly press the siding pieces into place. Start with the two shorter pieces and then attach the longer pieces. Let the wood glue dry for about 15 minutes. Using a drill, insert 1½" wood screws every 6" to fully secure the sides.

Step 3: Flip the whole bed over and dry-fit a swivel locking caster onto each corner, marking with a pencil where the screws need to go (see "Life Hack: Dry-Fitting" on page 83 for an explanation of dry-fitting). Remove the casters and drill a pilot hole into each mark. Put the casters back into place, and drive screws with your drill into the pilot holes. Flip the bed back over so the bed is caster-side down.

Step 4: Put on your vinyl gloves and stain all wood parts of the bed with a staining rag (you can use a sponge instead, but a staining rag offers more flexibility during application). Let the stain soak into the wood for about 5 minutes, and then wipe off excess with a clean rag. Let all the wood dry for 24 hours. Note: you do *not* need to stain the underside of the dog bed.

*4 wood boards for siding:
- small dog bed = two 2" × 4" × 30" boards + two 2" × 4" × 18" boards
- medium dog bed = two 2" × 4" × 36" boards + two 2" × 4" × 22" boards
- large dog beds = two 2" × 4" × 45" boards + two 2" × 4" × 28" boards

**piece of plywood:
- for small dogs = 20" × 30"
- for medium dogs = 24" × 36"
- for large dogs = 30 "x 45"

(continued)

LIFE HACK: WOOD STAIN

When working with wood stain, it's always a good idea to be in a well-ventilated area and to wear a mask. If you don't have an outdoor space to work in, be sure to open all windows and turn on multiple fans for good air circulation.

Step 5: Place your dog bed cushion on top. Bonus points if it matches the décor in your room! Lock the casters in place when your dog is using the bed and unlock and trundle away when it's not in use.

WORKOUT EQUIPMENT "CANED" CABINET

MATERIALS

- 2 pieces of wood (cut to fit like cabinet doors for the front of the bookshelf)
- jigsaw
- basic bookshelf (like the IKEA billy bookshelf)
- measuring tape
- pencil
- 2 sawhorses
- electric sander or sanding block
- wood casing (or molding)
- lincane aluminum sheet
- cutting shears
- staple gun + staples
- wood glue
- brad nailer + nails
- drill
- 2 self-closing concealed cabinet hinges
- 2 drawer pulls

Having a designated place to work out at home is a great way to build new healthy habits. For those shared spaces, like an office-workout room, having a place to store workout equipment is the ideal way to keep it looking like a gym during training hours but clean and office-ready during work hours. This cabinet hack will do both and take a basic bookshelf and turn it into a fabulous furniture piece.

Step 1: If you haven't done it already, cut your wood to size with a jigsaw, leaving you with 2 pieces that fit flush with the front and sides of the bookshelf. These are your future cabinet doors. (If you need help cutting wood, see our "Life Hack: Cutting Wood" on page 61.)

Step 2: Use a measuring tape and a pencil to mark a rectangle on each cabinet door that leaves 3" edges on all sides. Prop each cabinet door, one after the other, on top of 2 sawhorses and cut out the inside of each rectangle using your jigsaw. Sand all edges with either an electric sander or a sanding block for a smooth finish.

Step 3: Using a jigsaw, cut the wood casing (or molding) to outline the cut-out rectangles on the cabinet doors to look like a picture frame. Set these pieces aside.

Step 4: Roll out the lincane aluminum sheet and cut with cutting shears to fit the cabinet door rectangular cut-outs with 1" extra lincane on all sides.

Step 5: Using your staple gun, attach the lincane sheets to the cabinet doors, putting a staple every 2".

Step 6: Spread a thin line of wood glue on the back of the cut wood casing pieces and attach them on top of the stapled lincane edges. Let the wood glue dry for 15 minutes. Then, use a brad nailer to fully secure everything in place. Drive brads in at alternating 45° angles (rather than straight into the wood) along the wood casing.

(continued)

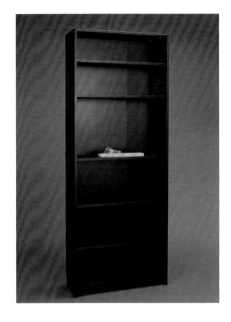

Step 7: Now it's time to attach the cabinet doors. Use a screwdriver or drill to screw two self-closing, concealed cabinet hinges into the inside sides of the bookcase and the back of each cabinet door. There should be one hinge 2" from the top, and another hinge 2" from the bottom.

Step 8: Add a drawer pull to the front face of each cabinet door. The easiest way to ensure that a drawer pull is installed straight is with this trick: Lay a piece of painter's tape on the back of the drawer pull. Use a nail to poke holes through the tape where the hardware screws need to be. Peel off the tape from the hardware and place on the cabinet door in the desired location. Drill screws into the marked spots on the tape. Peel off the tape and install the drawer pull on the door.

page
120

page
122

Laundry/ Utility Room

A laundry room or utility space is often overlooked as an area that can be creatively designed. Considering how much time it takes to do your laundry, do you really want to spend that time in a drab, depressing space? Function does not mean we have to completely give up on form.

Because this is inherently a smaller space than the rest of your home, it's the perfect opportunity to take a risk and go with a big, bold, and quirky pattern. Choose one wall as the focal point and then pick out a fun wallpaper that reflects your personality. Or maybe you want to get creative with color and paint a mural or a hand-drawn design. You'll actually want to do your laundry once you get your space looking good (hard to believe, but trust us on this one!).

Now, not all laundry room problems can be solved with color; smart storage solutions and practical prep space are equally as important. Baskets, lazy Susan turntables, glass jars—they are your new best friends. See our "ORGANIZATION 101: Proper Linen Storage" on page 200 for even more organization tips.

LAUNDRY SHELVES

MATERIALS

- drill
- spackle
- wood shelves
- level
- pencil
- wall anchors
- screws
- heavy-duty brackets and rod (optional)
- woven baskets
- glass apothecary jars

*One of the most common "builder-*grade" installs we see in utility rooms are those white, wire shelves. By upgrading shelving alone, you'll instantly achieve a custom look. If you have the space, consider installing a shelf with an attached rod underneath—great for hanging clothes. Be sure to purchase special brackets with rod inserts if you decide to go this route. Additionally, make sure you complete any painting or wallpaper installing before the shelves go in!

Step 1: Remove old shelving by using your drill to unscrew the old hardware. Cover up any holes with spackle (see "REPAIRS 101: Teach Me How to Spackle" on page 225 to learn how to spackle properly). Most spackle goes on pink during application and turns white to indicate being fully dry—this usually takes about an hour.

Step 2: Dry-fit your shelves to the wall in their desired locations (see "Life Hack: Dry-Fitting" on page 83 for an explanation of dry-fitting). Using a level to make sure they are straight, make a pencil mark where all new wall anchors and screws need to go. Set the shelves to the side. Drill pilot holes in marked spots and install wall anchors (see "Life Hack: Wall Anchors" on page 75). Securely attach the brackets by drilling screws into the wall anchors.

Step 3: Utilize your new shelves to the max by decorating with woven baskets and glass apothecary jars—random fabric cleaners and extra laundry supplies can go in the baskets, while pods or detergent can fill up the jars.

LAUNDRY HACKS

There are a million old wives' tales out there that give off-the-beaten-path advice for doing laundry. (For specific stain-remover tips, check out "Removing Stains from Textiles" on page 218.) Here's a list of hacks we stand by *and* call for items you probably already have on hand.

- Vinegar is your biggest secret weapon. Add a half-cup of distilled white vinegar to a load to remove lingering smells, boost softness, and restore whites to their original brightness. You can also soak smelly gym clothes in a white vinegar and cold water combo for an hour before washing—just let them air-dry, instead of using a dryer.

- Use wool dryer balls instead of dryer sheets. It's better for the environment, drying time will be cut down considerably, and you can add a few drops of essential oils to them every other month to make your laundry smell fresher.

- Use dishwashing detergent on grease stains before throwing them in the wash. Think about it—dishwashing soap gets grease off your pots and pans all the time! Scrub it into your clothes to help remove tough stains.

- Toss the plastic tops of liquid laundry detergent bottles in with the laundry to rinse off any residual drips. Remember to take it out before it hits the dryer.

- Line-dry your wash on a pool noodle to prevent massive creases. Cut the pool noodle to size, make a slit on one side, and maneuver it to fit comfortably on your drying rack.

- Tumble-dry your clothes with a couple of ice cubes on high heat for 10 minutes to remove wrinkles.

WALLPAPER/PAINT COMBO FOR A POP

MATERIALS

- degreaser
- paper towels
- painter's tape
- 2" shortcut polyester angle sash cutting brush
- paint (we like interior latex paint, eggshell-finish)
- 9" × ⅜" high-density pro woven roller brush
- peel-and-stick wallpaper
- measuring tape
- pencil
- level
- smoother tool
- X-Acto knife

Here's your chance to make a bold statement! If you're a renter, then peel-and-stick wallpaper is a great solution. Paint is ideal for both homeowners and renters alike. Why not combine the two for the ultimate impact? Pick a paint color that complements your chosen wallpaper. An easy way to do so is to find a color within the pattern and color-match it to the paint (your local hardware store can do the color-matching for you if you bring in a sample of the wallpaper). Your laundry room is about to get a whole lot more interesting!

LIFE HACK: CALCULATING HOW MUCH WALLPAPER TO ORDER

The best way to figure out how much wallpaper to order for a peel-and-stick project is to use a free wallpaper calculator tool online. Order 2 to 3 extra panels to make sure you have enough for your wall—you can always return extra unused, unopened packages after your project is complete!

Step 1: Disconnect your washer and dryer per the manufacturer's instructions and push them as far away from the wall as possible. Clean all walls with a degreaser and paper towels. Thoroughly dry.

Step 2: Use painter's tape to tape all edges of the focal wall (where the wallpaper will be going), plus the top of all baseboards. Use your cutting brush to paint all edges and corners, and then finish off the rest of the wall using your roller brush. Roll in a "W" pattern on the wall to evenly distribute the paint. Let the paint dry for 2 hours, and then do a second coat. Peel off the painter's tape once the second coat is complete, before the paint is fully done drying. Let the paint dry for another 2 hours before proceeding to the next step.

Step 3: Now we move onto wallpapering (see our "Life Hack: Installing Removable Wallpaper" on page 105 for instructions on how to properly install peel-and-stick wallpaper). Use the same X-Acto knife technique to cut around obstacles and windows. Keep hanging panels until the whole wall is covered.

Step 4: Reconnect your washer and dryer and push them back into place. Now you're going to be calling dibs on doing laundry, just to be in your cool new space!

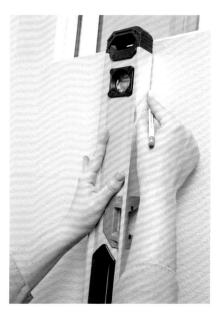

DESIGN 101

PILLOWCASE HAMPER ORGANIZER

MATERIALS

- 3 king-size pillowcases
- ruler
- chalk pencil
- painter's tape
- white fabric paint
- paintbrush
- 6 curtain grommets
- fabric scissors
- drill
- screws
- 6 decorative wall hooks

Make your laundry experience even easier by sorting your dirty clothes into these three labeled hampers as you go. It's the perfect blend of décor and utility, and when you're ready to wash, simply lift the hampers off the wall and dump them into the machine.

Step 1: Lay 1 pillowcase on a flat surface (iron out wrinkles if necessary). Using your ruler and chalk pencil, draw a top line, a bottom line, and a dotted middle line, each line spaced 3" apart. These will act as your straight edges for the labels. One pillowcase could say LIGHT, another could say DARK, and the third could say COLOR, or whatever is best for your laundry sorting needs. Maybe you'd rather label by family member name or soil level.

Step 2: Evenly sketch out each letter of the label, starting from the middle of the word and the middle of the pillowcase, and working outward—you'll get more uniformity and precision this way. Erase the straight-edge lines once the label is complete.

Step 3: Tape off the outline of each letter using your painter's tape (see our "Life Hack: Painter's Tape" on page 58 to learn how to tape off irregular shapes). Lightly paint on the white paint using the paintbrush. It's always better to do two lighter layers than to do one thick layer and risk having the paint seep under the tape. Once the letters are filled in with paint, remove the tape and let dry for 30 minutes.

Step 4: Your curtain grommets should come with a circle template. Use that to mark 2 circles at the top of the pillowcase—each circle should be 3" down from the top edge and 3" in from the right or left side, respectively. Cut out the center of the circle with fabric scissors and snap on the grommets.

Step 5: Repeat steps 1 to 4 with the other 2 pillowcases.

Step 6: Using your drill and screws, install the decorative hooks on the wall, 2 per hamper, at about 40" up from the floor. When hanging, the bottom edges of the pillowcases should lightly skim the floor. Now you can sort your dirty clothes according to the labels on the hampers!

LIFE HACK: AREA RUGS IN UTILITY SPACES

Rugs bring warmth to utility spaces. Use area rugs to warm up concrete and tile floors. So many area rugs are washable—some companies make it a point to tell you how washable their rugs are.

page
128

Outdoor Space

From a small balcony to a lush backyard, outdoor spaces are an extension of your home. They are such a terrific way to add more space, diversify your surroundings, and enhance your everyday life. Utilizing the outdoors can make any home an elevated space, and a great place to live.

Sometimes the problem you face is not knowing where to start with your slice of the Great Outdoors. And it can be overwhelming to walk into a hardware store or nursery and see the abundance of options before you. If you want to break it down, we recommend focusing on a place to sit, a few plants to adorn the space (see page 179 for some suggestions), and a few decorative items, like an outdoor rug, string lights, or a water feature.

Decide what works best for you and your family. Maybe that means a huge lawn for the kiddos and dogs to run around in with minimal décor distractions. Maybe you LOVE to entertain, so a patio with ample seating and lighting to set the party atmosphere is your jam. Keep in mind the climate you are in as well, and adjust plans accordingly to fit the weather and seasonal changes. Pretty soon your outdoor space will be your new favorite place in your home.

BALCONY BENCH

MATERIALS

- outdoor broom or pressure washer
- 8 (48" × 40") wood pallets
- 3" exterior wood screws
- drill
- circular saw or handheld hacksaw
- three 2x4s
- outdoor cushions

You can transform your balcony into a place you actually want to spend time on with this one project, which will create a love seat–size seating area. Wood pallets can often be found for free at furniture stores, liquor stores, or pet-supply chains. When shopping for outdoor pillows, look for specialty fabrics that hold up under the elements. You may spend a bit more money upfront, but they will last multiple seasons.

Step 1: Thoroughly clean your balcony, using an outdoor broom to sweep away all dirt and debris. For super-dirty spaces (no judgment here!), use a pressure washer.

Step 2: Set up 2 pallets next to each other vertically against the wall of your balcony to form the back of your bench. Lay down 2 pallets next to each other on the ground directly in front of the back pallets and drill wood screws through the ground pallets into the back pallets using your drill. Add a second layer of pallets on top of the ground pallets and drill a couple wood screws into the base every 4" for stability.

Step 3: Add the final layer of pallets and drive screws down every 4" to secure them to the pallets underneath and to the back pallets.

Step 4: Use a circular saw or a handheld hacksaw to cut the 2x4s to the same length as the side of the pallet base (about 40"). Layer 3 of the wood 2x4 cuts on top of each side of the bench to form armrests, and screw them into the pallets with wood screws at the front, middle, and end of the wood piece.

Step 5: Place outdoor cushions on top of your new balcony bench. To fully decorate your balcony, consider surrounding the pallet bench with potted plants and scattering a couple of decorative pillows on the bench. Grab a beverage and head outside to your new favorite spot—you're going to want to enjoy your first sunset on your refreshed balcony.

DIY YARD LOUNGER

MATERIALS

- iron
- 3 yards outdoor fabric
- ironing board
- fabric scissors
- sewing machine or needle and thread
- measuring tape
- pins
- 5 standard pillows

You might just spend your whole day outside, reading and lounging on this thing! This project is great for a backyard hang or to fold up the pillows and take it to-go and lounge on the beach. A sewing machine will make your start-to-finish time quicker, but hand-sewing with a needle and thread is certainly an option for those without access to a sewing machine!

Step 1: Iron the fabric on the ironing board and then lay it out flat on a table, pattern side facing down. Trim to 30" wide × 110" long, using your fabric scissors. Fold all sides down 1" and hem using a sewing machine. Lay out flat again.

Step 2: Grab the bottom edge, and fold up 28". Grab the top edge, and fold over. There should be about a 6" overhang. This will form the pockets for the pillows.

Step 3: Sew vertical seams to form 5 pillow pockets. Measure 20" in from the right edge (the width of a standard pillow), mark that point with pins, and use a straightedge to draw a straight line from the bottom of the folded fabric to the top. Sew a straight line at that marked point to join the fabric together to make a pillow pocket. From that sewn line, measure 20" and repeat the pillow-pocket sewing process. Continue until you have 5 pockets.

Step 4: Stuff pillows into each sewn pocket. Take outside and enjoy lounging in the sun (don't forget your shades!).

(continued)

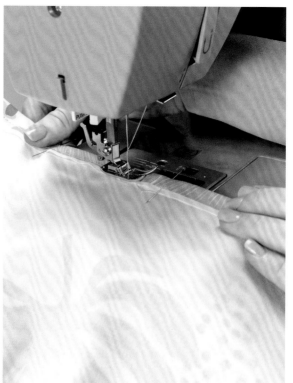

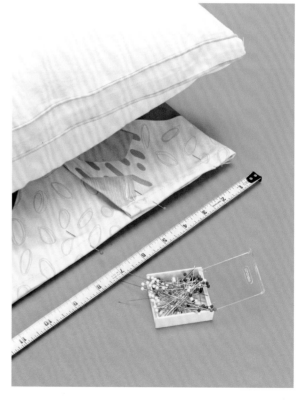

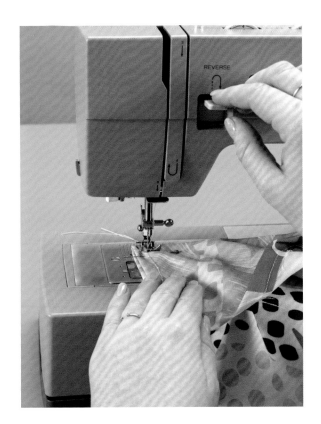

STENCILED OUTDOOR FLOORING

MATERIALS

- power washer (or soap and scrubber sponge)
- painter's tape
- flat-sheen exterior base paint
- 2" polyester angle sash cutting brush
- 18" textured roller brush with extension pole
- large tile stencil
- repositionable spray adhesive
- 6" dense foam roller brush
- paint tray
- colored paint for tile pattern
- stencil brush
- water-based spray urethane

There's nothing more depressing than an outdoor space not getting used to its full potential. Make it an area of your home that you love spending time in by starting from the ground up. If you're looking at a blank, smooth concrete patch in your yard or balcony, jazz it up by stenciling a tile look!

Step 1: Remove all dirt, dust, and debris from the area you plan on stenciling. The quickest and easiest way is with a power washer. You can rent those by the hour from your local hardware store. Or give it a good old-fashioned scrub with soap, water, and a scrubber sponge. Let the whole area dry completely.

Step 2: Using painter's tape, mask off any touching exterior walls or areas you don't want painted, like a column or a planter bed.

Step 3: Paint a base coat using exterior paint in a flat sheen. Paint the edges of the area with a cutting brush first. Next, you can use an 18" textured roller brush just as you would if you were painting inside. Cover the entire concrete area with paint. Let dry according to package instructions.

Step 4: Prep your tile stencil by spraying two coats of repositionable spray adhesive on the back and letting it dry for about 2 minutes. This will temporarily hold it in place on your concrete as you tile.

Step 5: Starting from the corner of the concrete area and working outward, place your tile stencil in position. Lightly load up the 6" dense foam roller brush with the colored paint, but be careful not to have too much paint on it. Using medium pressure, roll over the tile stencil. Use your stencil brush to fill in any textured areas that the foam roller may have missed. Peel off the stencil and move on to the next section, getting the tile in the correct position to repeat the pattern. Continue until the whole surface has been covered. Let dry according to manufacturer's specifications.

Step 6: Use your cleaned cutting brush to paint two coats of the water-based spray urethane along the edges of the concrete space. Then use the 18" textured roller to apply two coats of the water-based spray urethane to the rest of the concrete space. Let dry according to package specifications. This step will protect your paint from fading in the sun, and from rain or snow.

Step 7: Complete your new outdoor patio with comfy outdoor furniture and enjoy your new space!

LIFE HACK: TURF

Turf is looking *real* good these days. There are a lot of companies out there manufacturing extremely realistic turf, so consider installing it in place of maintaining live grass.

PART 2:

Get in There!

You've remade your space. You're happy with the rooms you've created and now it's time to use those spaces to relish all your hard work.

You've remade your space, and now it's time to use those spaces to relish all your hard work. Getting in there goes beyond great room design. It means filling your home with plants, hosting your loved ones for housewarmings or dinner parties, and taking pride in each space by keeping it organized. Signs of life—your life—that bring joy and make life worth living. Have the confidence to love the life you lead, with your home being a key reflection of that sentiment.

Follow our entertaining tips to decorate on the fly and throw an epic dinner party on a budget. Don't forget the plants! Not only are they pretty to look at, but they can improve the air quality of your home. Our "Guide to Being a Good Plant Parent" on page 170 will help you choose the right plants for both your indoor and outdoor spaces and teach you how to keep them thriving alongside you. Need help staying organized? Got you covered there, too. Let's get in there together.

page
152

page
155

page
158

page
162

Entertaining

Sharing your space is an extension of sharing your life with those you love. Opening your home to others is globally recognized as the fastest way to make friends and keep the ones you have. How you entertain in your space matters. Putting a bit of your own touch on your entertaining style tells the world who you are and how you care for others.

If you're reading this and thinking, "But I've never hosted a dinner party before," then this is your sign from the Universe! Take the pressure off about making things "perfect" and get excited about sharing the home you've worked so hard on. There are a lot of different ways to entertain. Maybe you want to throw a house rewarming party to show off all your refreshed rooms. Perhaps a dinner party is more your speed, complete with delicious food and wine and good conversation. Or you love to open your home to guests for days at a time and want to utilize that multipurpose room (see page 103) to its full potential. Whatever entertaining looks like to you, it can be the perfect excuse to get crafty and try a 101.

Here are some ways to go the extra mile to make your guests feel welcome and get the party started.

TASTEMADE'S FIVE GOLDEN RULES FOR ENTERTAINING

1. Create an atmosphere with a good playlist. Music can really set the tone for the evening and help get the party started.

2. Make a plan beforehand for your menu and have a few appetizers ready to be served when your guests arrive. Decide if food will be family style or individually served.

3. If guests offer to bring something, don't be afraid to be specific on what you need—or just tell them to bring wine.

4. Have fun at your own party! Don't stress if things don't go perfectly. The important thing is to be in the moment and make memories with your guests.

5. Send a quick "thank you" text or note to your guests afterward, thanking them for joining you.

VINTAGE TRUNK BAR CART

MATERIALS

- vintage trunk (find one made of wood)
- measuring tape
- jigsaw
- wood glue
- 2 MDF panels (cut to fit the sides of the trunk)
- clamps
- paintbrush
- white paint
- 4 corner braces
- drill
- short ½" screws
- level

Having a stocked bar cart brings the party to any room. This DIY can look cool and set you up for a successful evening of entertaining. Depending on your preference and lifestyle, you can stock the trunk to the nines with ingredients for cocktails *and* for mocktails. Swap some of the liquor bottles for sodas and garnishes.

Step 1: Open up the vintage trunk and remove any existing contact paper. Clean if necessary.

Step 2: Measure 2" in on all edges of the front of the trunk's lid and remove that panel, using your jigsaw, and set aside. The edges of the trunk should remain intact, as well as the locking mechanisms.

Step 3: Apply a liberal amount of wood glue to the back of one of the MDF panels and press the panel firmly onto the side of the trunk. Repeat on the other side. Clamp each side and allow the glue to dry fully, which usually takes about 45 minutes. Once dry, close what remains of the trunk lid and slide the trunk lock or latch into place.

Step 4: Measure the inside of the trunk from side to side to determine shelf length. Use the jigsaw to cut the front panel piece into one shelf piece to size. Paint the inside of the trunk and the shelf with white paint and let dry according to paint manufacturer's specifications.

Step 5: Install the corner braces into the inside of the trunk, two for each side of the shelf, using your drill and a few 1½" screws. The shelf should be a snug fit—you may need to knock it into place. Use a level to make sure it's straight.

Step 6: Set your new bar cart up with a wine rack on the bottom, large bottles and glassware on the shelf, and a decanter or two sitting on the very top of the trunk itself. Have extra coasters stored in there as well to be the real MVP host.

(continued)

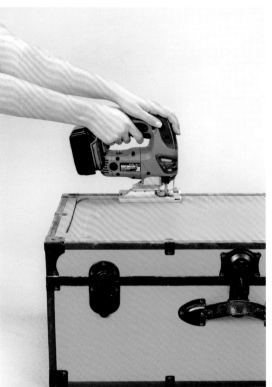

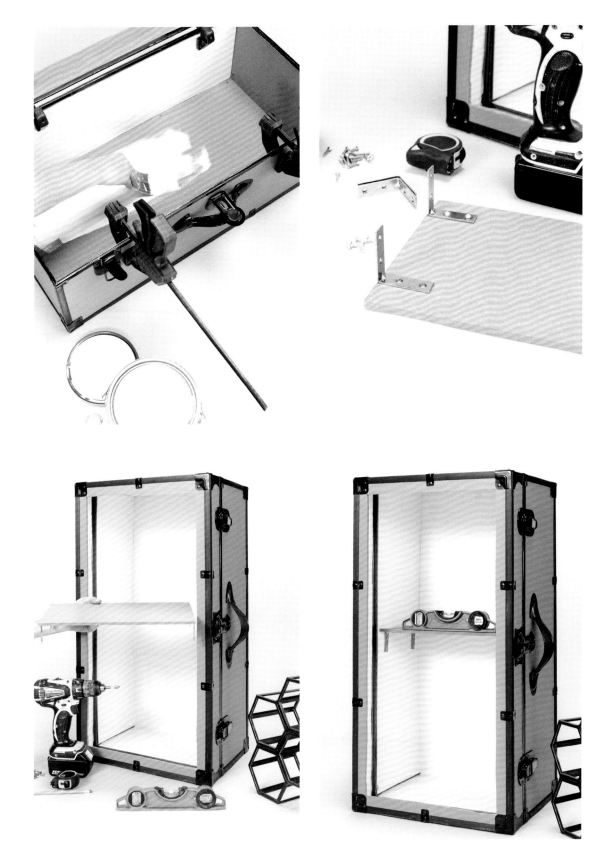

WOOD BLOCK CANDLE CENTERPIECE

MATERIALS

- multiple taper candles of different heights
- drill
- spade bit
- 4" × 4" × 24" wood base (if you can, use a reclaimed wood block)
- 100- to 120-grit sandpaper

Set this centerpiece out before guests arrive or leave it up to enjoy all by yourself—we won't blame you for wanting to admire your masterpiece! Go bold with your candle colors to get a color explosion effect or keep it neutral for a softer look. The variety of taper height will give it dimension and texture either way. Bonus points for making your own twisted candles (see page 155)!

Step 1: Count out your candles—that's how many holes you'll be drilling. Using your drill and spade bit, start drilling holes directly into the top of your wood base. Choose spots to drill at random for more of a whimsical look. You want the holes to be about 2" deep (which is deep enough to support a tall taper).

Step 2: Take a bit of 100- to 120-grit sandpaper and hand-sand over the tops of the holes, just enough to remove any splintered sections.

Step 3: Insert a taper into each hole, playing around with height variety throughout the piece. Place this centerpiece on your table and light it up!

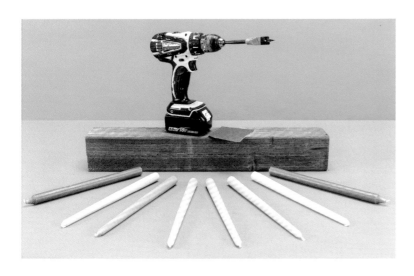

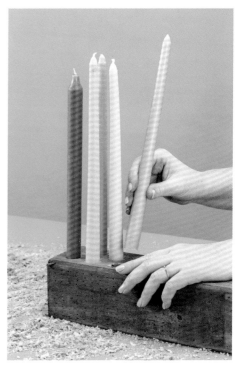

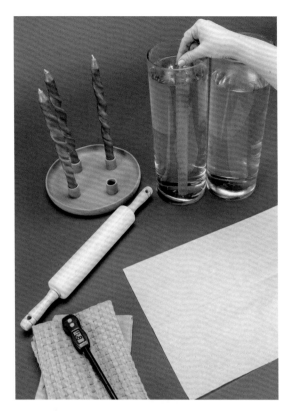
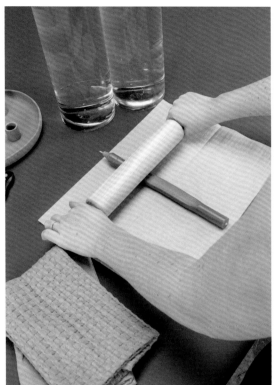
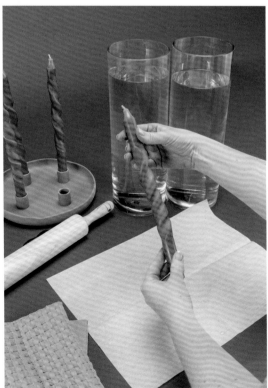

TWISTED CANDLES

MATERIALS

- 2 tall 14″ containers
- food thermometer
- taper candles
- wax paper
- rolling pin
- dish towel

Twisted candles make for a fun weekend DIY and will add awesome pops of color to your tablescape. The key to making this project work is to get the proper water temperature. Too hot and your candles will melt away completely. Too cold and they won't become pliable. Display them in a cool candlestick holder for a décor focal point.

Step 1: Fill one container with cold water and the other container with water heated to 104°F. Pro tip: The best way to ensure proper water temperature is to use a food thermometer. Put a taper candle in and wait 15 to 20 minutes.

Step 2: Take the candle out and place it on top of a piece of wax paper. Lightly roll it out with your rolling pin. To achieve a spiral-twist-look like the one pictured here, be sure the candle is relatively flat.

Step 3: Using both hands, quickly twist the taper into shape. It should look like a spiral staircase! Place the candle in the other container, filled with cold tap water, for about 5 minutes.

Step 4: Remove the candle from the water and dry it off with a dish towel. Repeat until all tapers are twisted.

UPCYCLED BOTTLE VASES

MATERIALS

- wine or beer bottles
- yarn (in an array of colors)
- masking tape
- 2" nylon paintbrush
- découpage glue
- scissors
- flowers or greenery

Throwing a dinner party on a budget?

Upcycle old wine, beer, or soda bottles with this crafty trick for a colorful table setting that will WOW your guests. Soak them in water first and peel off any labels. Look for a variety of bottle heights to give your table centerpiece dimension.

Step 1: Clean out the inside of your bottles and let them dry completely.

Step 2: Choose your starting yarn color and tape it to the bottom edge of the bottle, with the tape going vertically.

Step 3: Brush a small amount of découpage glue next to the tape and begin pressing the yarn to the bottle, adding more découpage glue as needed. Continue until the entire bottle is covered—you can swap in other colors of yarn to make a pattern as you go. When you reach the top, snip the yarn close to the edge and secure with a dot of découpage glue.

Step 4: Repeat with as many bottles as you'd like to make a beautiful tablescape. Add flowers or greenery to complete the look.

TIE-DYE NAPKINS

MATERIALS

- **6 plain white cloth napkins**
- **rubber bands**
- **1-gallon plastic bin**
- **rubber gloves**
- **7-ounce bottle of dye**
- **dishwashing liquid**
- **salt**

Tie-dye harkens back to the days of summer camp and middle school art class—oh the nostalgia! Elevate this technique to adult status and set your table in style with this satisfying DIY. If you prefer to do an ombre pattern, follow the instructions for "DESIGN 101: Ombre Curtains" on page 88—just swap out the curtains for napkins!

Step 1: Take a napkin and accordion-fold it first, then fold each side into the middle to create a small rectangle.

Step 2: Add rubber bands at random to the rectangle. The more rubber bands, the more complex the pattern on the finished napkin. Set aside.

Step 3: Pour boiling water into the 1-gallon plastic bin. Put on your rubber gloves. Add ¼ bottle of dye to the water (we like to combine colors like clementine and fuchsia),

a dollop of dishwashing liquid, and a dash of salt. Stir to combine.

Step 4: Drop the folded and banded napkins into the dye mixture, making sure they are fully submerged. Soak for 5 minutes.

Step 5: Remove the napkins from the dye mixture and take off all the rubber bands. Run the dye-soaked napkins under cold water until the water runs clear. Wash in the washing machine in cold water. (Be sure to run a "clean" cycle afterward to clear out any traces of dye.) Let them air-dry. Iron before using.

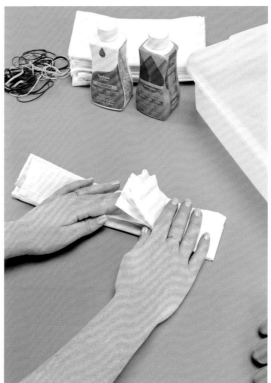

CONFETTI TRAY

MATERIALS

- wood tray
- découpage glue
- 2" artist's brush
- colorful paper confetti (bonus if it has glitter mixed in)
- tape measure
- pencil
- 3 cups resin + hardener
- 2 pull handles
- drill
- wood screws

Try to find a more festive party tray than this one—we dare you! Keep the party going by turning a plain wooden tray into a confetti concoction, perfect for holding drinks and pitchers to serve your guests with ease.

Step 1: Brush the bottom of your wood tray with découpage glue using your artist's brush, making sure to cover the entire surface liberally.

Step 2: Sprinkle with paper confetti until you've achieved a thick layer on the bottom of the tray. You shouldn't see any of the wood or glue peeking through.

Step 3: Attach a pull handle to each side of the tray using your drill and wood screws.

Step 4: Mix the resin and hardener per package instructions and pour a resin layer on top of the confetti layer. Make sure it thoroughly covers all confetti pieces. Let harden completely according to manufacturer's instructions.

Step 5: Pop the bubbly and pour a glass of champagne to celebrate!

SAVORY BAR

MATERIALS

- a variety of pretzels and dipping sauces
- 5 small bowls
- twine
- scissors
- decorative metal arch
- paper clips
- paper to-go sleeves
- stamp + ink pad

Make your meal interactive by setting up a fun food bar! It's a great way to keep the flow of the party going and creates conversation starters for your guests. Plus, it gives people the ability to create their perfect snack. For a savory option, consider laying out a pretzel bar. Those salty knots of goodness taste delicious dipped in just about anything.

Step 1: Offer a few different types of pretzels to lend visual appeal to your pretzel bar. You could serve classic twisted pretzels, nuggets, sticks, or knots.

Step 2: Lay out the bowls and fill each with a different dipping sauce. Beer cheese, honey-mustard, ranch, melted blue cheese, and BBQ sauce are all tasty options.

Step 3: String up twine between the sides of a decorative metal arch. Tie the edges into a bow to mimic the shape of the pretzel. Untwist paper clips and use them to hang up the pretzels on the twine line.

Step 4: Provide paper to-go sleeves as a courtesy. You can find blank ones online, and then stamp each one with a custom design to really go the extra mile.

"GO THE EXTRA MILE"
GUEST BASKET

Have you ever been to a boutique hotel or short-term rental that included a personalized touch to greet you when you arrived? Why not take a page out of their book and make your own! It doesn't have to be much, but the gesture alone will start your guest's stay off on the right foot. Here's what you can include in a "Go the Extra Mile" Guest Basket: fresh towels, the Wi-Fi password in a cool frame, a small sprig of rosemary or lavender tied up with string, a water bottle, a chocolate bar, a candle with matches, and, for a personalized touch, something local that represents your hometown. If there's a cool brewery your area is known for, you might include a bottle of their most popular beer. Maybe your town makes the most incredible butter molds. Random or unique touches are conversation starters and it's always great to support local businesses. Put all these items in a large wicker basket and leave the basket at the foot of the guest bed.

SWEET BAR

MATERIALS

- wooden pillar candlesticks
- drill
- spade bit
- 120-grit sandpaper
- food-safe spray paint
- extra-strength wood glue
- 12" wood dowel
- a variety of desserts (including doughnuts)
- paper to-go sleeves
- stamp + ink pad
- glass jars and trays (in a variety of shapes and sizes)

You and your guests will be riding that sugar high all night long after sampling from this sweet food bar option. Just be sure to grab your favorites—they probably won't last long!

Step 1: To make a DIY doughnut stand, drill a hole into a wooden pillar candlestick with a drill and a spade bit. Sand the edges of the hole with 120-grit sandpaper until smooth. Spray paint the base with a fun color and let dry according to package instructions. Put a few drops of extra-strength wood glue into the bottom of the hole and insert a wood dowel. Let dry completely (about 1 hour) before stacking doughnuts on top of one another on the dowel.

Step 2: Provide paper to-go sleeves so your guests can load up on their favorite sweets. Stamp the front of each sleeve with a custom message to your guests.

Step 3: Set out a variety of shapes and sizes of glass jars. Artfully fill them with candy, brownies, or cookies.

DIFFICULTY LEVEL 2

"KEEP THE SETTING" PARTY FAVORS

MATERIALS

- a variety of vessels (e.g., teacups, votives, glass jars)
- bouquet of flowers
- scissors
- cardstock
- marker
- hole punch
- twine

A party favor isn't always necessary, but it is a sweet surprise for your guests. This hack doesn't require you to break the bank, and it provides a personalized touch to make your guests feel valued and welcome. Bonus: You won't have anything extra to clean up because at the end of the night, your guests will take their place setting home.

Step 1: Head to your local thrift or secondhand store. Browse around and find teacups, votives, or small glass jars—be sure to buy one for each of your guests (plus a few extras in case of unexpected guests!). Pick up a bouquet of your favorite flowers on the way home.

Step 2: Fill up each vessel with a little bit of water and place a single cut flower inside. It should look like it's just floating on the surface.

Step 3: Cut out place cards from nice cardstock and use a marker to write each guest's name on a card in your best handwriting. Punch a small hole in the corner of each place card, and tie a card to each of your thrift store finds with twine.

Step 4: Set your table and place each unique setting by its proper seat.

Guide to Being a Good Plant Parent

Buying plants is easy. Taking care of them is the hard part. Plants range from the indestructible to the needy. Which kind of plant parent are you? Do you want high-maintenance plants that require a watering schedule or would you rather pick plants that only need care once a month? Is this your first foray into plant purchasing or are you a seasoned horticulturist? Let's run down a list of both indoor and outdoor plants, where they should live, and what you will need to keep them thriving.

INDOOR

These plants are some of our favorites and make any room feel more inviting and pulled together. There have been studies that show that an environment including natural elements brings a positive outlook on life and helps people feel more alive and active. Plus, plants look great. It's a win-win in our book!

KEY

SUNLIGHT

LOW   MEDIUM   BRIGHT INDIRECT (I) OR DIRECT (D)

WATER

INFREQUENT   NORMAL   FREQUENT

ENVIRONMENT

DRY   NORMAL   HUMID

WARM   COLD

DIFFICULTY

1 BEGINNER   *2* INTERMEDIATE   *3* ADVANCED

Snake Plants

Oh, the plant-that-can't-be-killed! This is the perfect plant to start with. Some snake plant tags will literally say "best if left alone." And they aren't kidding. You'll only need to water it every 10 days or so (at most). They like to dry out completely between waterings. The most common mistake with a snake plant is overwatering! The other good news is that these plants can survive in both direct and indirect light. You'll be hard-pressed to find an easier plant to take care of.

LIFE HACK: FAKE PLANTS
Fake plants are great for those who want the visual impact of plants without the necessary care. Just remember to dust them regularly!

Orchids

The 1940s were considered the golden era of the orchid, thought of as one of the most glamorous accessories to an outfit or a hairstyle. The iconic image of Billie Holiday comes to mind. These days, orchids are experiencing a serious resurgence of popularity in home décor. Contrary to popular belief, taking care of orchids is quite easy! Here's a watering hack—about once a week, place three ice cubes at the base of your orchid and let them fully melt. The slow absorption of water is the best way to avoid overwatering. Even though orchids like a warm, somewhat humid environment, do not place them in direct sunlight. After blooming, you can repot them in fresh orchid soil, as well as snipping off the old stems at their base. With proper care, your orchid plants can last for months and months, allowing you time to fully enjoy this beauty in your home.

Rubber Tree

If you want to add color variation to your plant collection, consider a rubber tree. With its beautiful burgundy leaves, this plant is easygoing and great for beginners. Rubber trees thrive in medium indirect light, so stick yours close to a window with a sheer curtain to ensure proper sunlight exposure without it getting blasted. A good balance of water every 10 days or so is key. The soil should not be too dry or too wet. Stick your finger in the soil if you're unsure about a good watering time. If the top layer is totally dried out, and the underlayer is damp, then it's time to lightly water. A word of caution: Rubber trees are extremely toxic to humans and pets if consumed, so keep them out of reach of small children and fur babies.

Chinese Money Plant

This adorable plant (also called pilea) looks amazing in minimalist or Scandinavian-inspired designs. Thought to bring good luck and good fortune, it's a fun plant to bring to a housewarming or to give as a gift. Pilea can be hard to find in stores but are very easy to propagate (learn how to propagate in "Growing from Cuttings" on page 185), so if you have a friend with one of these already, bring over a bottle of wine in exchange for a cutting and grow your own. Chinese money plants like bright, indirect sunlight, and it's recommended to rotate your plant each time you water it, so that all sides benefit from the sun. It should never have soaking-wet soil and only needs some water once a week. If its leaves start to droop, give it some water and they should perk right back up.

Monstera

You may have heard this plant called by its nickname, the Swiss cheese plant. Either way, this is a gorgeous addition to any home and will be sure to be a showstopper in your plant collection. These plants come in a range of prices, with 2-foot or 3-foot ones ringing in around $50, and larger or variegated plants selling for upwards of $150. There are even super-rare ones on the market for over $5,000! They like bright, indirect sunlight (but not right in front of a window). More light means more frequent watering, whereas lower light requires less, but on average your plant will need to be watered every 1 to 2 weeks. Let the soil dry out completely in between waterings. Overall, it's a pretty easygoing plant (not to mention, super photogenic). Snap those photos and jump on the Monstera trend!

Indoor Succulents

There are quite a few varieties of succulents to choose from and they are all relatively easy to care for! Some favorites of ours to start with are burro's tail, jade plant, aloe vera, and Mexican snowball. Plant them individually, or all together in one planter, like our "DESIGN 101: Succulent Coffee Table" on page 50. The good news is that even if you forget to water them, these plants will still survive!

Pothos

Another great beginner plant, pothos is like the chameleon of the plant world. This very low-maintenance and forgiving plant would look awesome in a hanging planter or on a shelf. You shouldn't even have a watering schedule for pothos; rather, check for when the soil feels too dry and add water. (A quick note: Keep pothos away from cats and dogs, as ingesting the leaves can be toxic to these animals.)

LIFE HACK: DUST YOUR PLANTS
Dust or wipe down the leaves of your plants every few months using a soft microfiber cloth. This helps to keep your plant looking fresh and beautiful!

Fiddle Leaf Figs

Fiddle leaf figs get their name from the distinct "fiddle" shape of their leaves. They can be pretty pricey, often costing between $100 and $200, so this is a plant best for a confident plant owner who's well-versed in fiddle leaf care. They'll need to be in a fairly temperature-controlled room and almost directly in front of a window that gets a lot of bright, indirect sunlight. Once you've found its happy spot, DON'T MOVE IT!! Fiddles are creatures of habit, and once they settle into an environment they love, they will thrive. Rotate your plant each time you water it, so that all sides get equal amounts of sunlight. The most common ways to kill a fiddle leaf fig are to overwater it or let it get too dry. The best practice is to water it fairly heavily about once a week.

OUTDOOR

These plants are a great complement to any outdoor space (check out the Design 101s in our Outdoor Space chapter on pages 127 to 141). We like to use them in large-scale planters on patios and balconies, providing a backdrop for the rest of the design and a visually interesting vignette for your eye to rest on. Some of them have flowers for pops of color, while others just smell incredible; either way, your senses will be tingling, and you won't want to come inside!

Jasmine

This elegant vine-like plant is a gorgeous addition to any outdoor space and has the potential to look awesome and smell even better. One of the coolest ways to incorporate jasmine into your life is in a diamond-patterned trellis on a side wall of your home. You can build your own ("PLANTS 101: Diamond Garden Trellis," page 192) or buy a small one from the hardware store. Secure it to the wall, plant the jasmine, and then train its vines to grow using training wire or by weaving it directly into the trellis. Have a little patience, and by the next year you'll have a stunning feature wall in your garden. Jasmine prefers semi-shady spots and highly fertilized soil. Keep this plant well cared for by watering it regularly and vigilantly training the vines to grow the right way. Italian villa vibes, anyone?

Bougainvillea

If you want to enjoy beautiful, bright flowers nearly year-round, and you live in the proper, temperate climate, then bougainvillea is the outdoor plant for you. You'll see this plant all over the place in arid climates like southern California and northern Mexico and it is a terrific addition to any outdoor space. There's a variety of sizes of bougainvillea that can be grown as hedges, over a trellis, against a building, or as ground cover. Once fully established in the ground, these plants are actually quite easy to care for. Be sure to place your plant in a sunny spot, as bougainvillea needs at least 6 hours of full sun. Not enough sun means not a lot of color on your plant. They are pretty drought-resistant, too—you'll just need a solid watering every 3 to 4 weeks. Overwatering means more greenery and fewer flowers, and since the bright flowers are the star of the bougainvillea show, try to avoid that at all costs. If you're training your bougainvillea to grow on a building or arbor structure, be sure to provide proper support, like a trellis and/or training wire.

Boston Ferns

These leafy plants look fantastic in planters and grow really fast. The best practices for ferns are to leave them in the shade—too much sunlight and they will shrivel up and die fairly quickly. Ferns are high maintenance and have to be attended to every single day. You never really need to dump water into your fern planter; instead, get in the habit of spritzing it daily from a spray bottle.

LIFE HACK: FERTILIZING

Fertilizing is an easy step in your plant care routine. Simply purchase a bag of fertilizer from your local nursery, add a layer on top of your plant, and water thoroughly. This should be done every 4 to 6 weeks for outdoor plants, depending on the specific plant.

LIFE HACK:
Consult experts at your local nursery to pick plants that will survive all year round in your environmental zone.

Strawberries

Can you think of anything more delicious than a freshly grown strawberry, plucked right from your very own garden? They are surprisingly easy to grow, and you can pick from a variety of ways to do so. We like the three-tiered, raised-planter look. Strawberry plants get little runners that look like vines—this is how they spread out and grow—so be sure to pick a planter that has extra room. They can handle cool temperatures and a light frost, so strawberry planting season can happen in early spring or early fall. When you first come home from the garden center, soak the strawberry roots for about 20 minutes to rehydrate; then, plant them in super-hydrated, nutrient-rich soil. They love the sun (as do most berry plants!), and you'll want to water them weekly at the root. Once they get that rich, red, berry color, they are ready to be harvested. Any berries that don't make it into your belly should be refrigerated.

Outdoor Succulents

Hardy succulents, like agave, aloe, and echeveria, are ideal for outdoor gardens. When cared for correctly, they can thrive in many different climates. Too much water will kill succulents, so you need to make sure they're planted in well-draining soil. A trick is to make a 6-inch mound of succulent soil mix and then plant your succulent in that. If you would rather plant in a planter, terra-cotta is a perfect match. The benefit of going the planter route is that you can bring your plants inside during heavy rains or snow. Their watering schedule changes with the seasons; a good rule of thumb is to water them thoroughly once a week in the summer, twice a month in the spring and the fall, and once a month during the winter.

Citrus Potted Trees

A potted tree is the perfect way to add drama and privacy to your outdoor space. Because a potted tree is inherently tall, it can be a great focal point in your garden or terrace, with smaller potted plants and outdoor features clustered around it in a luscious vignette. Bonus: Citrus trees do great in containers *and* pull double duty by providing you with freshly grown fruit! The key is ensuring that the pot is large enough, with a drainage hole, and, in the case of a citrus tree, consider adding a small plant lattice for growth support. Look for dwarf varieties for your potted trees so that they thrive in a container. Watering is super important, as potted trees dry out more quickly than ground-planted ones, so stick to a strict watering schedule. Make sure to fertilize regularly (see "Life Hack: Fertilizing" on page 181), and after a few years, plan on repotting your tree in a new container that's slightly deeper and wider.

GROWING FROM CUTTINGS

Friends let friends have plant cuttings. Also known as "propagation," this is a fun way to create new plants in your home, using cuttings from already established adult plants. It's also fun to start "trading" cuttings with friends and grow your houseplant collection without spending a cent! All you need to get started is an adult plant and a glass jar with water. Easiest propagation plants include: pothos, philodendron, African violets, spider plants, and prayer plants.

- First, look for a root node on the main plant. It looks like a mini stick sticking out the side of a stem. Using a sharp knife or scissors, cut about ¼" below the node.

- Place the cutting in a glass jar filled with room-temperature water. Make sure it's filled high enough to cover the root node.

- Change the water every 3 to 5 days, lightly washing off the bottom of the cutting each time to get rid of any bacteria or grit.

- Wait and watch for roots growing from the bottom of the cutting. When they've reached 3" to 5" it's time to transfer the cutting to soil. Word to the wise: Have patience during this process! It can take anywhere from a few weeks to a few months for the roots to grow long enough, depending on the type of plant.

MEDITERRANEAN-INSPIRED HERB CONTAINER GARDEN

MATERIALS

- wine barrel planter
- drill with ¼" drill bit
- plastic trash bag
- rocks
- gardening gloves
- potting soil
- fertilizer
- trowel
- a variety of herbs (we are using lavender, thyme, basil, tarragon, rosemary, and oregano)
- watering can

Whether you're a city dweller or a rural resident, container gardening is a great way to flex your green thumb. You'll get the chance to grow plants that might not naturally grow in your region and control the environment by moving your container around to get optimal sunlight. Even better, you can grow your own food! Talk about sustainable living. First things first: Choose your container. You can use just about anything for this, but it's a good idea to avoid dark or metal containers, as they can get very hot in the sun and cook your plant's roots. For this project, we'll be using a half–wine barrel planter for a Mediterranean-inspired herb garden.

Step 1: Drill four or five drainage holes in the bottom of the wine barrel planter, using your drill and a ¼" drill bit. Good drainage is key to keeping your plants alive. Place the planter in a spot with full sun.

Step 2: Line the bottom of the planter with a plastic trash bag and poke holes to align with the drainage holes drilled in step 1. Fill with rocks to hold the trash bag in place. Fill up the remainder of the planter with potting soil. If it's not already mixed with fertilizer, be sure to thoroughly mix fertilizer in.

Step 3: Plan out where your plants will go. You don't want to crowd your container. Visually it's a good idea to put taller plants in the middle and shorter plants closer to the rim of the planter.

(continued)

LIFE HACK: PROTECTING YOUR CONTAINER GARDEN

When hard weather (like heavy rain, snow, or sleet) hits, make sure your container garden is protected! If your container is too heavy to move inside, place 4 yardsticks directly in the dirt at four corner points of the container and drape a tarp to cover the whole vessel. If your container garden is easily movable, bring it inside until the storm passes.

Step 4: Plant your herbs! Using your trowel, create an appropriately sized divot for each plant—each should be just a few inches wider than the herb itself. After the plant has been placed in its divot, pack down the topsoil to secure the plant in place, and soak with water to allow it to settle into its new home. Moving forward, avoid overwatering, as this will be a quick way to kill your herb garden. When it rains, allow the soil to fully dry out before resuming your usual watering schedule. During the hottest summer months, you may need to water twice a day.

Step 5: Break off the leaves or cut 3" sprigs of fully grown herbs to use while cooking. Your recipes will be instantly elevated with delicious, homegrown herbs.

MAKING YOUR OWN COMPOST/ CONTAINER SYSTEM

MATERIALS

- garden waste
- food waste
- shovel
- tarp

There are many reasons that composting is a good idea. One, it's good for the environment to reuse your food waste and reduce the carbon footprint you leave on the planet by keeping these materials out of landfills, thus helping to minimize greenhouse gases. Two, composting results in super–nutrient-rich soil that will help your garden flourish. When learning which foods are best for composting, a good rule of thumb is this: If it can be eaten or grown in a field or garden, it can be used for composting. Here's a more comprehensive list of what to compost: fruits and veggies, eggshells, coffee grounds and filters, tea bags, shredded newspaper, cardboard, paper, yard trimmings, grass clippings, houseplants, hay and straw, leaves, sawdust, wood chips, hair and fur, fireplace ashes. If you only have indoor space to work with, it's best to purchase a special composting bin from the gardening store. As long as you keep track of what you're throwing in, it shouldn't smell or attract pesky pests. If you have an outdoor area, here's the best way to get your compost pile going.

Step 1: Pick a dry, shady spot, close to a water source, or within reach of your garden hose.

Step 2: Add garden waste—like yard trimmings and wood chips—as it's collected. Break up any larger pieces. Water down the dry materials as they are added to the pile.

Step 3: Once this base has been established, begin mixing in food waste, like fruits and vegetables, making sure to bury them under 10" of garden waste, using your shovel. Cover the pile with a tarp to hold in the moisture.

Step 4: When the bottom of the pile reaches a dark, rich color, it's considered properly "composted." Use just the dark compost from the bottom of the pile for your garden and continue adding to the top. The entire process can take anywhere from 2 weeks to 2 months.

Step 5: Sprinkle compost on the top of outdoor garden beds, blend it with potting soil for houseplants, or rake it over your lawn. Whichever way you choose to use it, your garden will thank you by happily growing during blooming season.

DIAMOND GARDEN TRELLIS

MATERIALS

- measuring tape
- marking chalk
- ladder
- hammer (for brick exteriors) or drill (for wood/siding exteriors)
- masonry nails (for brick exteriors) or eye hooks (for wood/siding exteriors)
- work gloves
- galvanized wire
- wire snips
- shovel
- 6 (10") grower pot flowering vines of your choice (we're using jasmine in this example)
- fertilized soil
- garden ties
- 3 planter boxes (optional)

There is something romantic and whimsical about flowering vines trailing up the side of a building. If you have a blank wall on the exterior of your home, this is the perfect 101 to transform the entire area. Remember to purchase the proper nails for your exterior! If you have brick walls, use a masonry nail. If you have wood or siding, use eye hooks. The rest of the process is the same!

Step 1: First, use your measuring tape to determine the desired overall width of your trellis. Let's use a 9-foot-wide wall as an example. Using your marking chalk (which can be washed off with water), mark the ground at 1 foot and 8 feet. These will be your two end points—you want them each 1 foot in from the end points of the wall, so the jasmine has room to spread out and grow. Mark the middle point at 4½ feet for a total of three marks.

Step 2: Use your measuring tape and chalk to mark 6" inches up from each of the three ground marks. If you have a brick wall, hammer a masonry nail into a mortar joint closest to your measured-out marks, leaving about half of the nail exposed. If your exterior is made of wood or siding, drill an eye hook into it instead, leaving the circular hook exposed.

Step 3: Adjust this next step according to your desired trellis height—let's use a 7-foot-tall wall as an example. Starting at one of the two end points you marked on the ground, measure 7 feet up and make a mark—this will be the top of the wall. Then, starting from the same mark on the ground, measure 3½ feet up and make another mark—this will be the middle point of the wall. Make both of these marks above the other end point you marked on the ground as well, but make only one mark above the middle ground mark, at 7 feet up from the ground. Hammer a masonry nail or drill an eye hook into each mark on the wall. There should now be eight nails or eye hooks in total.

(continued)

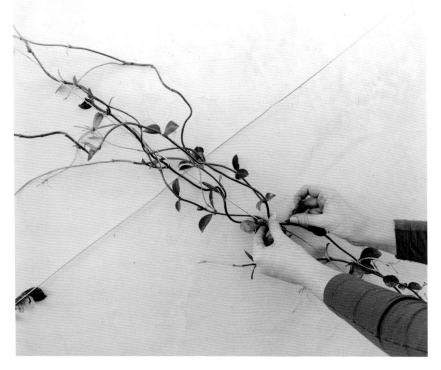

Step 4: Put on your work gloves for this next step, as you'll be handling the galvanized wire. Starting at the bottom-left nail, wrap the wire around the nail or eye hook 3 times. Then pull the wire spool up to the middle-left nail or eye hook above, keeping the wire taut, and wrap the wire around the nail or eye hook 3 times in a clockwise direction (this secures it in place). Continue pulling the wire and wrapping it around all the nails or eye hooks until you've formed a square. Once you've made your way back to the bottom-left nail or eye hook, wrap the wire around it again and pull the wire diagonally toward the upper-right nail or eye hook. Wrap the wire around the upper-right nail or eye hook 3 times and then cut the wire, using your wire snips.

Step 5: Wrap and secure a new piece of wire around the bottom-right nail or eye hook. Pull and extend the wire all the way to the upper-left nail or eye hook. Wrap the wire 3 times around that nail or eye hook and then cut the wire.

Step 6: Wrap and secure a new piece of wire around the bottom-middle nail or eye hook. Pull and extend the wire to the middle-left nail or eye hook. Wrap 3 times before pulling and extending to the upper-middle nail or eye hook. Wrap 3 times before pulling and extending to the middle-right nail or eye hook. Wrap

3 times before pulling and extending back down to the bottom-middle nail or eye hook. Securely wrap the wire 3 more times before cutting.

Step 7: Now it's time to plant your vines! Using your shovel, dig 6 holes as close to the wall as possible: one on either side of the bottom-left nail, one on either side of the bottom-right nail, and one on either side of the bottom-middle nail. Plant your jasmine vines, one in each hole. Use fertilized soil to fill in the dug hole around the newly planted vine. Optionally, use three large planter boxes if you don't want to dig directly into the ground.

Step 8: Take each tendril of the vine and gently wrap it around the galvanized wire, securing with garden ties if the vine doesn't naturally stay wrapped. Continue wrapping up the trellis pattern. Over time, as your vines continue to grow, the whole diamond pattern will be filled with new vine growth. Encourage the vines to stay with the galvanized wire by wrapping as needed and securing with garden ties. Make sure to water frequently and fertilize as needed.

LIFE HACK: CHOOSING THE RIGHT VINE

Check with your local garden center to pick the best vine for your region, climate, and home's sun exposure. Just be sure to choose something in the vine family, as it's the easiest type of plant to train to grow in a diamond-shaped pattern!

page
200

Organizing

We've all been there. The doorbell rings
with unexpected company and your house is a mess. You race across each room, stuffing random things into junk drawers, shoving dirty laundry into the closet. Great cardio, but not great for your sanity. The best way to avoid this whole scenario is to put in place a good organization practice. Having everything in its designated space sets you up for success, but getting the ball rolling can feel like moving a mountain. Remember: Take it one space at a time. Start in your pantry. Work toward your linen closet. End with your clothes closet. One refresh in front of the other will result in a pretty and organized home.

The first thing you've got to do is a major purge. There's no use trying to organize when there's too much stuff to work with. Take a day and thoughtfully go through your items—have you used it in the last year? Does it still function properly? Do you still genuinely like it? If it's hard for you to let things go, shift your focus to the person who could benefit from your unused items. Donating gently used clothing and household items should be part of your seasonal cleaning schedule (see page 217). If an item carries sentimental value, then you absolutely should keep it, even if it's not necessarily "practical." But otherwise? Use it or lose it.

MAKING THE MOST OUT OF YOUR FOOD STORAGE

MATERIALS

- shelf liners or contact paper
- a variety of glass or plastic containers
- chalk marker
- Command strips
- wire baskets
- tiered stadium storage
- lazy Susans

It's lunchtime. You open up your pantry and it seems like you have *nothing* to eat. The truth is, there is probably a full meal in there—but if you can't actually see what you have, then your pantry is not working for you. Having an organized pantry will save you money and reduce food waste. This is a great weekend project!

Step 1: Pull everything you have out of your cupboards and throw away any expired food. Wipe down all shelves and lay down shelf liners or contact paper.

Step 2: Raid the dollar store for a variety of glass or plastic containers. Pour dry goods like cereal, pasta, rice, sugar, and flour out of their original packaging and into their respective containers. Label each container with a chalk marker, writing directly onto the plastic or glass.

Step 3: Using heavy-duty Command strips, hang wire baskets on the pantry walls—these are perfect for onions, potatoes, and garlic. Hang them in a column with a 12" gap between baskets.

Step 4: Invest in tiered stadium storage for your canned goods. Each time you shop, pull the older cans forward to the front row, and stock the back rows with the new goods. This will help utilize all vertical space in between shelves and help you remember to eat all your canned goods before they expire.

Step 5: Put in a few lazy Susans for your spices, oils, and sauces. Rotate the lazy Susans to check what you've got before heading out to the store.

Step 6: Remember to go through your pantry once a month to organize it and toss any expired food. Add it to your cleaning schedule (see page 217) so you don't forget!

ORGANIZING 101

PROPER LINEN STORAGE

DIFFICULTY LEVEL 1

MATERIALS

- baskets
- fabric storage bags
- labels
- marker

A well-organized linen closet makes your life easier and extends the life of your bedding. The ideal scenario would be to open up your storage space and know exactly where everything is. Here are a few tips to actually make that dream a reality.

Step 1: Go through all your linens and sort them into piles—all the queen-size bedding in one pile, all the towels in another, all the seasonal bedding in another, and so forth.

Step 2: Match up each complete set of sheets and fold together into a bundle, with the fitted sheet on the bottom, then the top sheet, then the pillowcases. This is a great time saver because when you need to change the linens on your bed, you can pull out a full set at once. Bonus: Set up an individual basket for each bed size (e.g., a "twin-bed basket").

Step 3: Donate any items that don't have a complete set and purge non-essential or worn-out linens.

Step 4: Roll your bath towels and stack them in a basket. Same with your hand towels and washcloths.

Step 5: Zip up seasonal items in fabric storage bags to protect them from dust and moths, and store them on the top shelves. Your easy-to-reach shelves should hold the items you use regularly.

Step 6: Label each basket to help quickly identify what goes where and to help with the organizational upkeep. Life happens and you get busy, so do everything you can to set your home up for success.

FOLDING A FITTED SHEET

Folding a fitted sheet deserves a tip all unto itself. Yes—there *is* a proper way to fold, and no, it's not just bunching it in a ball and throwing it in your linen closet (we've all been there . . .). Follow these steps and your fitted sheets will look as pretty as the day you bought them.

- Put your hands in the top corners on the long side of the sheet, inside out.

- Bring your hands together and fold the right corner over the left one. Pull the sheet taut and switch your right hand into the corner. Use your other hand to straighten the edges.

- Your left hand now goes in the other corner. Stretch out both hands again and repeat the process.

- Now you should have a rectangle, with your left hand in the corner, and your right hand on the straight-edge side. Lay the rectangle down on a clean and flat surface with the edges facing up.

- Fold the top down a third lengthwise, and the bottom side up to meet it. Then, fold into thirds again, going from the left to the right. You did it! Yay adulting!

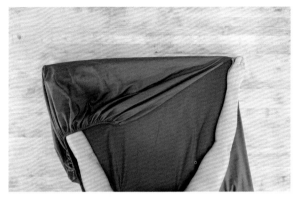

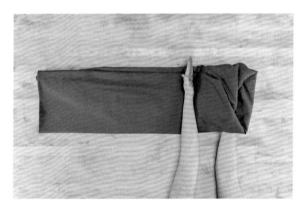

CLOSET ALTERNATIVES

MATERIALS

- painter's tape
- paint
- 2" polyester angle sash cutting brush
- 6" roller brush
- stud finder
- ladder
- wood shelves (with brackets installed)
- measuring tape
- drill
- screws
- wall anchors
- level
- wooden dowel rods
- matching hangers
- small bench or ottoman
- faux sheepskin rug
- woven basket
- oversized floor-length mirror

Some apartments or older homes simply don't come with closets. The quickest solution is to purchase a wardrobe (and, while you're at it, check out our "DESIGN 101: Custom Wardrobe Upgrade" on page 99). But we have another closet alternative solution that is perfect for the weekend. Your room will look like a custom boutique, and you'll have no choice but to keep it neat and tidy. If you mostly wear neutrals, pick a rich moody paint color to help them stand out. If bright patterned colors fill your wardrobe, opt for a softer neutral wall paint.

Step 1: Using painter's tape, mask off the trim, baseboards, and edges of the wall. Start the painting process by using your cutting brush to paint the edges and corners, and then fill in the rest of the wall using your roller brush (see "REPAIRS 101: Prepping to Paint a Wall" on page 226).

Step 2: Use your stud finder (see "Life Hack: Finding a Stud" on page 37) and mark where each stud is on the wall. We're going vertical to optimize space, so get ready to hang those shelves high, at around 50" from the floor, so you'll need your ladder to reach the top-most points. Using your drill, aim to drill most, if not all, of the brackets directly into studs. Use wall anchors on any holes that don't hit those marks (see "Life Hack: Wall Anchors" on page 75 to learn how to install wall anchors properly). Always use a level to ensure that your shelves are straight. These are now your shoe racks! Organize your shoes neatly, with the heels facing out to make them easy to store and grab.

Step 3: Hang up the wooden dowel rods using the brackets that came already installed under the shelves. Make your clothing look as tidy and clean as possible by using matching hangers.

Step 4: Use your purses and overnight bags as additional storage by stuffing them with scarves and sweaters and placing them on the floor underneath your hanging clothing. Having these bags stuffed with clothing will help them retain their shape when they're not in use. Baskets or bins work just as well!

Step 5: Add a small bench or ottoman next to the hanging clothes if you have the room and layer a faux sheepskin rug on top for extra coziness. Slide a woven basket underneath the bench and use it to store seasonal items.

Step 6: Prop an oversized floor-length mirror on an adjacent wall to bounce more light around the space and give you an opportunity for a full outfit check.

LIFE HACK: THINK VERTICAL

Hang your hats on the wall, as high as you can reach. Build shelves high up at the tops of all closets, and stack labeled bins and boxes up there with seasonal items, freeing up space at eye level for your daily items. Install a pegboard in your kitchen to hang pots and pans and cooking utensils. Utilize under-the-bed storage bins, and behind-the-closet-door storage racks.

TABLETOP ORGANIZATION

MATERIALS

- various large trays
- coffee table book
- planter with fresh flowers or a plant
- set of coasters
- sculptural object of your choice

Trays are your new best friend. Tabletop organization can be applied to any desktop, workspace, coffee table, or vanity. Picture a random collection of items in your living room scattered across the coffee table. Looks cluttered, right? We can fix that with a few easy steps.

Step 1: Find a large tray that fits comfortably on top of the coffee table. Pick one that is a different material than the table itself, like a bronze and mirror tray on top of a wood table, or a black metal tray on top of an acrylic table.

Step 2: Place a coffee table book—like this one (Hint! Hint!)—inside the tray.

Step 3: Add a short planter with either fresh flowers or a plant to the tray. Another option would be to place the tray either to the side of or on top of the coffee table book.

Step 4: Stack a couple of coasters next to the coffee table book, all still within the tray. Remotes can be placed on top of the coasters or off to the side.

Step 5: Depending on how much room you have left, add a sculptural object that makes you smile. Maybe it's a trinket you picked up while traveling. Or maybe it's a funky bowl. Because it's all contained within the tray, your coffee table is packed with personality without looking cluttered.

PART 3

Keep It Up!

Guess what is just as satisfying as decorating your home? Organizing and maintaining it.

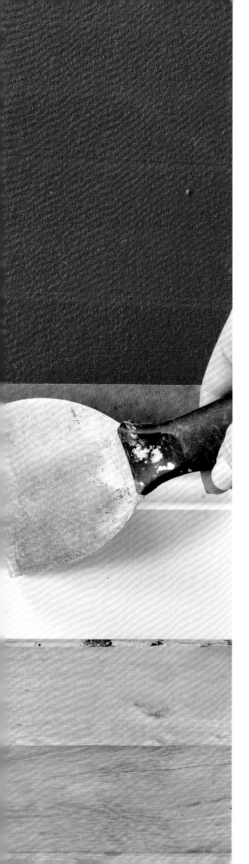

Refreshing your space is just the beginning of your home journey. Once you're done, it will be your job to keep it gorgeous, organized, and well-maintained. Listen: There are certain things we don't recommend touching without getting an expert involved. For instance, don't change your plumbing if you don't plumb (words to live by). However, there are scads of simple upkeep techniques you can learn that will keep your space in great shape for a very long time to come . . . or until your next refresh.

Get an upkeep routine going and make an event out of it. Crank up the music and pop the top of your favorite beverage. It's an empowering feeling to know how to do work around your own house. It's the little details, like having small holes filled in from old hanging artwork, or your baseboards repaired and clean. Things that creep up over time to make a house feel worn can easily be fixed and give your home a fresh makeover feeling. Think of this section as your quick reference guide to adulting (are we still using that word??). It may not be glamorous to learn how to, say, load your dishwasher properly, but it's so important to extending the life of your appliances, dishes, and, ultimately, your wallet.

Your well-loved home will love you right back if you keep it up.

page
216

Maintenance: Cleaning

Maintaining your refresh is more than just keeping up with the big things. It's making sure that the details of your home stay well taken care of so that you don't have to worry about them. Here's the best news about learning how to properly clean your home—once you've learned it once, it will be a skill you can carry with you for the rest of your life.

The biggest tip is to get on a schedule with your cleaning. Literally, mark your calendar with what you're aiming to accomplish that week. This way the dust, dirt, and debris won't creep up on you and feel overwhelming *and* you'll get that awesome sense of achievement by getting to cross that cleaning task off your to-do list once it's completed. Just so you know, a lot of people struggle with this. You are not any less accomplished because your house is messy. But at the end of the day, it feels good to be in a clean home. You've already spent all this time with your refreshes, so be proud of your space by upkeeping it.

DISHWASHER CLEANING

MATERIALS

- bowl
- distilled white vinegar
- baking soda

It may feel silly to clean a dishwasher when it's constantly cleaning dishes (like . . . wouldn't that just . . . clean it??), but you'd be surprised at the grime and soap scum that can build up over time. Add "dishwasher cleaning" to your cleaning schedule on a monthly basis.

Step 1: Remove any visible food debris and throw it away.

Step 2: Place a bowl full of distilled white vinegar on the top rack and run a HOT wash cycle. The vinegar helps blast away grime, dissolves soap buildup, and sanitizes the whole machine.

Step 3: Toss a handful of baking soda along the bottom of the dishwasher and run a short HOT wash cycle. Baking soda is a great deodorizer and stain remover, so your dishwasher will be left looking and smelling clean.

THE RIGHT WAY TO LOAD A DISHWASHER

Let's talk about the right way to load a dishwasher. There actually *is* a correct way to load yours (you can win that argument with your roommate now . . . you're welcome), and by following this guide you'll have cleaner dishes and avoid unnecessary dishwasher breakage.

- Scrape food off dishes and pre-rinse them before adding them to the dishwasher. Place dirty dinner and salad plates facing the same direction on the bottom rack—they should never go on the top rack.

- Add larger pieces like mixing bowls and casserole dishes to the sides of the bottom rack and avoid placing them facedown—this can block the sprayer from reaching the top rack. Do not overload, as this prevents thorough cleaning, and you'll get stuck having to hand-wash a lot of dishes.

- On the top rack, stack small bowls so that they face the middle. Place glassware facedown in a neat row. Don't try to cram glasses in there if they don't easily fit—this can lead to breakage.

- For utensils, load forks and spoons faceup, and mix them together so that spoons don't stick to one another. Knives should always go facedown, so you don't cut yourself while unloading. Spatulas and ladles should lie flat on the top rack (rather than being placed in the utensil holder).

- Add dishwasher detergent. Run hot water in your kitchen sink for a few minutes before pressing START on the dishwasher (this will help heat the cleaning water to its proper temperature at the start of the wash cycle). Select the appropriate wash setting, depending on how dirty your dishes are (any dishwasher made within the last 10 years will be able to do a lot more specific tasks than you might think!).

- These items should *always* be hand-washed: wooden spoons, sharp knives, cast iron, delicate dishware like china or crystal, nonstick pots/pans.

MAKE YOUR WINDOWS SHINE

MATERIALS

- 2-gallon bucket
- 1 tablespoon liquid dishwashing detergent
- sponge mop with pole extension
- squeegee
- microfiber cloths
- ladder

Wait until springtime with warm weather for this annual cleaning task. Cold weather will potentially freeze the liquid dishwashing detergent and water mixture to your windows and no one wants to deal with that mess! Your windows will sparkle and shine after this project, the perfect welcome when you walk up to your home.

Step 1: Fill your bucket with cold water (about 2 gallons) and mix in the liquid dishwashing detergent.

Step 2: Dunk your sponge mop in the water mixture and use it to scrub the outside of your window to cover the whole piece of glass.

Step 3: Use your squeegee to clean the window, starting on the left side and working toward the right with horizontal strokes. Wipe off the squeegee with your microfiber cloth between each pass.

Step 4: For second-story windows, use your ladder and the pole extension on your sponge map. Repeat until all the windows are cleaned.

DEEP-CLEANING YOUR OVEN

MATERIALS

- baking soda
- glass jar
- sponge
- rubber gloves
- 2 cleaning rags
- spray bottle
- distilled white vinegar

This certainly isn't our favorite chore, but it is a necessary one. Ovens can get pretty grimy. Maybe that late-night pizza cheese dripped down and burned to a crisp on the oven floor or grease from a holiday ham spilled all over. Now is the time to clean it all up and get your oven looking and smelling good as new. No one needs a smelly kitchen!

Step 1: Turn off your oven, make sure it's completely cool, and remove the oven racks. Start this 101 in the evening after you're done cooking for the day.

Step 2: Mix together 2 parts water to 1 part baking soda in a glass jar to form a paste. Use a sponge to cover the entire oven with the paste. We recommend wearing rubber gloves for this part as it can get quite soot-y in there.

Step 3: Let the paste sit in place in the oven overnight. In the morning, wipe all of the paste out with a cleaning rag. The baking soda helps to lift off any crusty burnt remnants inside the oven.

Step 4: Fill a spray bottle with distilled white vinegar and spritz the inside of the oven. Let it sit for about 30 minutes. Wipe down the oven with a different cleaning rag. Put the oven racks back in.

CLEANING 101

DIFFICULTY LEVEL 1

A QUICK MICROWAVE-CLEANING SOLUTION

MATERIALS

- ½ lemon
- microwave-safe bowl
- pot holders
- paper towel

From sauce splatter to butter explosions, using a microwave can get messy. This hack takes less than 10 minutes and uses items you probably already have in your kitchen. Bacteria can grow and spawn from old food spills left in the microwave. Wipe it down after each use and rotate this cleaning hack in once a week.

Step 1: Place half a lemon facedown in a microwave-safe bowl. Fill with water until about half of the lemon is submerged. Place the bowl in your microwave.

Step 2: Microwave on HIGH for 4 minutes. The essence of lemon will work magic on the grease and grit built up in your microwave.

Step 3: Let the lemon bowl sit for 1 minute before removing it from the microwave. Careful—the bowl might still be hot! Use pot holders as a precaution.

Step 4: Wipe away all stains with a paper towel. Everything should wipe away as easy as butter sliding off a hot frying pan. Bonus: Now your kitchen will smell like lemon!

CLEANING SCHEDULE

We can all agree that being in a clean home is nice. But can we also agree that sometimes it's hard to maintain? Following a cleaning schedule is a great way to keep you from being overwhelmed. How do you climb a mountain? One step at a time!

MONDAY

○ sweep & mop floors

○ do one load of laundry

TUESDAY

○ dust

○ clean mirrors

○ do one load of laundry

WEDNESDAY

○ clean bathrooms

THURSDAY

○ clean out fridge

○ make a grocery list

○ wash all towels

FRIDAY

○ vacuum

○ wash sheets

SATURDAY/SUNDAY

○ do grocery shopping

○ put out fresh flowers

DAILY

○ make bed

○ empty & load dishes

○ pick up & put away clutter

○ wipe counters

○ put away clothes

○ take out trash & recycling as needed

MONTHLY

○ deep-clean inside of appliances (oven, fridge, microwave, washing machine, dishwasher)

○ wipe down all cabinetry

○ scrub backsplash/grout

○ vacuum baseboards & vents

○ wash windows

○ dust doors & walls

○ disinfect garbage cans

SEASONALLY

○ clean out expired food in the pantry

○ wash drapery/blinds

○ clean out closets

○ wash comforters

○ wash carpets

REMOVING STAINS FROM TEXTILES

It happens to the best of us. You're eating sushi and you look down and realize you've dribbled soy sauce down the front of your favorite shirt. Ugh. While it may feel like your night is ruined, have no fear—your clothing is *not*. The same is true for your home goods. While you can't always throw something in the washer, like drapes or a rug, there are tons of ways to treat spills. Remember: Always test out the stain-remover solution on a less visible section of fabric before doing any stain-removal procedure. Here are a few of our favorite tricks for getting pesky stains out of textiles.

Soy sauce: Mix together 1 part laundry detergent to 2 parts distilled white vinegar to 3 parts cool water. Apply to the stain with a scrubber sponge or by dabbing it with a cloth. Let it sit for 10 minutes. Rinse with cool water and repeat until the stain is gone. Blot with a cloth to air-dry.

Red wine: Club soda is the easiest way to remove red wine stains from clothing or carpet. Pour a liberal amount onto the stain and allow the carbonation to fizz and break up the color. Then dab with a clean cloth until the stain is gone. For larger stains, sprinkle table salt over the stain immediately to lift the color, then add club soda. Refrain from scrubbing, as this will only drive the stain further into the textile.

Coffee: Blot the stain with a clean cloth immediately. Mix together warm water, ½ teaspoon dishwashing detergent, and 1 tablespoon distilled white vinegar. Presoak the stain in this mixture for about 15 minutes. Rinse with warm water and let air-dry.

Sweat: Mix equal parts lemon juice, water, and salt, and scrub the stain. Rinse with cold water and let air-dry. For tough sweat stains on white fabrics, spray on fabric bleach and let sit for 30 minutes before washing with cold water.

Grease: Run the stain under cool water. Add liquid dishwashing detergent and scrub into the textile. Let air-dry to make sure the stain is gone before throwing it in the wash.

Makeup: Spot-treat with liquid dishwashing detergent by dabbing with a clean cloth. Hand-wash with hot water in the sink while lightly scrubbing out the stain.

Ketchup: Turn the fabric inside out and rinse with cold water. Scrub with distilled white vinegar and a clean cloth to get the stain out; then wash as usual.

Vinaigrette: Run just the stained part under cold water. Dab liquid dishwashing detergent onto the stain. Add a few drops of distilled white vinegar. Rinse under cold water, lightly rubbing the fabric as you do so. Repeat until the stain is gone, and then toss in the regular wash.

> ### LIFE HACK: PREVENTING PERMANENT STAINS
> High heat from your dryer will permanently set most stains, so be sure they're gone before tossing them in.

YUP, CLEANING YOUR WASHING MACHINE IS A THING

MATERIALS

- toothbrush
- hydrogen peroxide
- clean cloth
- 1 to 2 cups distilled white vinegar
- ⅓ cup baking soda

Akin to cleaning your dishwasher (see page 212), learning how to clean your washing machine is very important. Soap residue and minerals from the detergent you use to wash your clothes build up over time and coat the inside of the laundry drum. Mold buildup is also a possibility. Ever wonder why your clothes stopped smelling so fresh after a wash? Not having a clean machine could be the culprit! Note: These steps are for a front-loading washer. (See "Life Hack: Cleaning a Top-Loading Washer" opposite for how to clean a top loader.)

Step 1: Open the front door of your washing machine. Dip a toothbrush in a small cup of hydrogen peroxide and scrub around the rubber gasket to remove any mildew or mold.

Step 2: Wipe down the glass front of the door with a clean cloth dipped in distilled white vinegar.

Step 3: Pour 1 to 2 cups of distilled white vinegar into the liquid detergent dispenser.

Step 4: Run your machine at the hottest cycle. The vinegar should thoroughly knock off soap scum and water buildup.

Step 5: After the vinegar cycle is complete, open the front-loader door and add ⅓ cup of baking soda to the inside of the machine. Run another cycle at the hottest setting. The baking soda acts as a deodorizer. Your washing machine should look clean and smell great—plus, your clothes will come out cleaner than ever.

LIFE HACK: CLEANING A TOP-LOADING WASHER

It's easy to clean a top-loading washing machine with this simple process. Start the wash cycle and fill your machine with hot water. Stop the cycle once the machine is full and add 3 cups of distilled white vinegar. Stir to combine. After letting the water/vinegar mixture sit for about an hour, run a normal wash cycle.

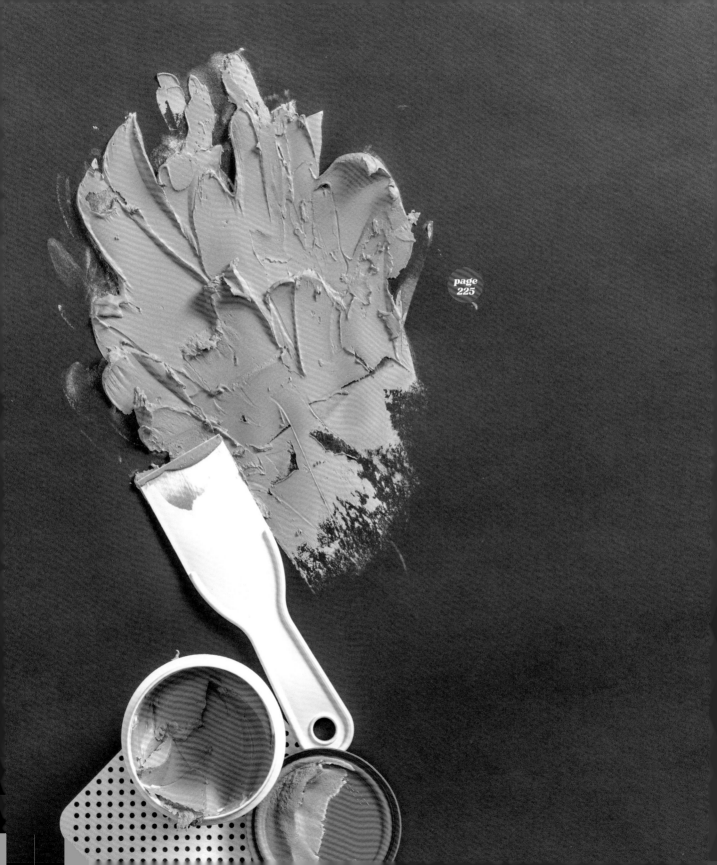

page
225

Maintenance: Repairs

You can save a lot of money in the long run if you learn how to do basic home repairs on your own. As we mentioned before, don't take on a task above your skill set! But even more advanced skills can be learned over time. Repairing your home will also set your designs up for success. Slapping paint over a hole in the wall will only make the hole look more pronounced (we've learned this from personal experience . . .). Learn how to repair those imperfections first, and your designs will stand out as if a professional had done them.

If you've been following along with the 101s in the rest of this book, you should already have a lot of the materials needed for these repairs on hand (see "Tool Kit" on page 14 for suggestions). Things like spackle, sandpaper, or wood glue can be used in a variety of home-repair projects. Your repairs will be completed in no time at all, and your house will look great!

WALNUTS AREN'T JUST FOR EATING

MATERIALS

- whole shelled walnuts
- clean cloth

This is one of those urban myths that actually works. It's incredible that something as simple as a walnut can make your floors and wood furniture look new again. Here's the secret: The natural oils from the walnuts seep into the wood, helping heal those nasty scratches.

Step 1: Take a whole walnut and rub the meat of the nut thoroughly into the scratch in the wood. Rub for a couple of minutes to really work the oils in.

Step 2: Wait about 15 minutes, and then wipe off any excess oil with your clean cloth. Done!

TEACH ME HOW TO SPACKLE

MATERIALS

- spackle spatula
- spackle (we like the kind that goes on pink and turns white when dry)
- mesh tape patching
- scissors
- 180-grit sandpaper
- wall-texture spray

If you're worried about the potential drywall damage that comes with mounting a TV or hanging art and shelves, don't be! With spackle in your arsenal, your walls will look as good as new when old art comes down or when you move out. Even holes as large as 2″ can be repaired with this miracle product. Remember to spackle before repainting!

Step 1: Identify minor holes (under 1″ wide) in your walls that need to be spackled. Use a spackle spatula to apply spackle directly to the holes and smooth it into place. If a hole is particularly deep, you may have to use 2 to 3 layers of spackle. Wait until each layer dries completely before applying the next one. (A lot of spackle brands go on bright pink but turn white to indicate that they are fully dry.)

Step 2: For holes wider than 1″ (but not exceeding 2″), add spackle around the perimeter of each hole using your spatula. Place a piece of mesh tape patching (use scissors to cut to size) over the entire hole and add more spackle to secure it in place. Let this layer fully dry, and then apply another layer of spackle to cover the entire piece of netting. Smooth the edges into the wall, using the spatula.

Step 3: Once your spackle has fully dried, hand-sand down the edges and bumps with 180-grit sandpaper. When you run your hand over the patched hole, it should be smooth and flush with the wall.

Step 4: A lot of walls are textured (this varies by region), so a smoothed-out spackle patch may stand out. Apply a thin layer of the appropriate wall-texture spray on top of the repaired hole. Let the product dry according to package instructions. Now you won't be able to tell where the hole was in the first place!

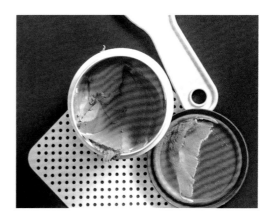

PREPPING TO PAINT A WALL

MATERIALS

- duster
- all-purpose cleaning spray
- clean cloth
- painter's tape
- caulk + caulk gun
- 2" polyester angle sash cutting brush
- primer
- 6" roller brush
- paint tray

Painting the walls of your home is one the easiest and most affordable ways to personalize your space. Paint can make a huge difference in the "feeling" of a room. It lends itself to the design style you gravitate toward and is easily changeable if you'd like to redecorate in a few years. Prepping your walls for paint often takes longer than the painting itself, but it's an essential step to take for a professional-looking finish.

Step 1: Use a duster on all surfaces you're about to paint on or around, then clean them with all-purpose cleaning spray and a cloth. Have you ever checked the tops of your door frames? It gets pretty gross up there. Without cleaning first, all that dust and debris will mix into your paint, leaving it looking streaky and discolored. For any holes that need filling, learn how to spackle on page 225.

Step 2: Use painter's tape to mask the trim, baseboards, crown molding, light-switch covers, and windows. For a crisp paint line, use the caulk trick (see "Life Hack: Caulk Trick" on page 85).

Step 3: Use your cutting brush to apply primer to all edges, corners, and crevices. Fill in the remaining wall space, using your roller brush and a paint tray. If you're painting over a light color and the paint you select is actually a paint and primer combo, you can skip this step! But if you're painting over a dark color or using a paint product without primer mixed in, include this step in your prep process.

Step 4: Let the primer dry according to product specifications (a few hours will usually do the trick). Now that your walls are prepped and primed, you're ready to paint!

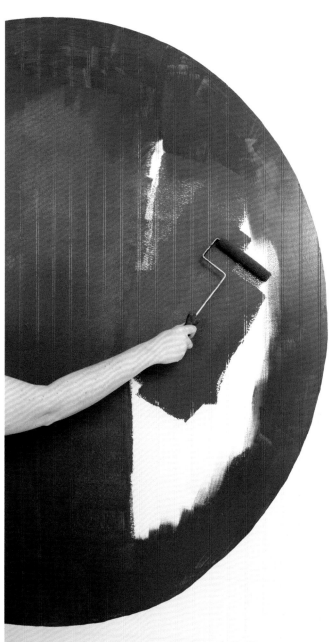

CRACKED-TILE REPAIR

MATERIALS

- rubbing alcohol
- clean cloths
- wood glue
- nail polish (that matches the tile color)
- cotton swab
- nail polish remover

If you have a small fracture in your bathroom or kitchen tile and don't feel like replacing the whole thing, give this 101 a try. This hack works for both hairline and wider cracks. When finding a nail polish color to match your existing tile, try combining two colors to get an exact match.

Step 1: Clean the entire tile area with rubbing alcohol and a clean cloth. Make sure it is completely dry to the touch before moving on.

Step 2: Squeeze wood glue to fill in the crack fully. Use your finger to smooth it out, wiping off excess onto a clean cloth. Let the wood glue dry fully, about 30 minutes.

Step 3: Paint on the nail polish with the small paintbrush attached to the polish bottle. Make sure the entire crack is covered, even going a smidge over the line to seal the repair. Let the polish dry completely for about 15 minutes.

Step 4: Dip the cotton swab into the bottle of nail polish remover and remove any excess nail polish around the crack. Apply light pressure to lift up stubborn polish.

Step 5: Wipe down the whole area with a clean cloth.

THE DOG ATE MY BASEBOARDS

MATERIALS

- 120-grit sanding block
- scissors
- wood filler (we like the kind that comes in a tube)
- clean cloth
- painter's tape
- 2" polyester angle sash cutting brush
- primer
- paint or stain (the same color as your existing baseboards)

Okay, okay, we totally threw dogs under the bus; cats are fully liable here, too (although cat damage may be more of the scratch/clawing variety). Either way, your wood baseboards have been damaged, and you need to fix them! This 101 is great for minor repairs and will leave your wood baseboards looking brand-new.

Step 1: Use your 120-grit sanding block to remove any splinters from the damaged part of your wood baseboards.

Step 2: Use scissors to snip off the top of the wood filler tube, about ¼" down from the top and at a slight angle. Squeeze the tube to apply a liberal amount of product to the damaged hole or area. Let it dry completely—you'll know it's dry when it feels as hard as the wood.

Step 3: Sand off any excess wood filler until it's flush with the surrounding baseboard. Use a clean cloth to wipe away dust or debris.

Step 4: Place painter's tape on the wall above the baseboard (see "Prepping to Paint a Wall" on page 226). Use your cutting brush to apply a layer of primer over the repaired baseboard area. Let dry for 1 hour.

Step 5: While the primer is drying, clean your cutting brush thoroughly in the sink. Run it under hot water and massage the brush to get under all the bristles. The water will run clear when the brush is clean. Squeeze out the water and let the brush dry on a flat surface for 1 hour.

Step 6: With your clean (and dry!) cutting brush, paint over the repaired area. Let dry according to paint manufacturer's specifications.

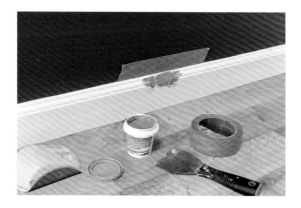

HARDWOOD FLOOR FIX

MATERIALS

- sawdust or wood shavings
- spare cardboard
- wood glue
- 220-grit sandpaper
- clean cloth

Once, when prepping to hang a piece of art on the wall for a *Weekend Refresh* shoot, we drilled a hole in the wood floor . . . oops! Instead of freaking out and worrying that we had ruined the floor, we used this hack. This is a terrific idea for holes smaller than 1". Anything bigger we'd recommend bringing in a professional.

Step 1: Collect sawdust or wood shavings from previous 101 projects—basically any project that you needed to cut wood for would have produced sawdust or wood shavings. Use those!

Step 2: On a piece of spare cardboard, squeeze out a dollop of wood glue. Use your finger to mix a liberal amount of sawdust or wood shavings in with the wood glue until a paste is formed.

Step 3: Push the paste mixture into the hole in the floor until it's completely filled in. Wait about an hour for the wood glue to fully dry.

Step 4: Take your 220-grit sandpaper and hand-sand down the paste, moving the sandpaper in the direction of the wood grain of your floors. Clean up any wood dust with a clean cloth.

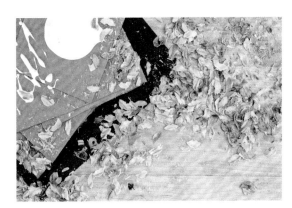

Acknowledgments

Special thanks to the members of the Tastemade team and our *Weekend Refresh* episode designers, whose creativity, hard work, and support made this book a reality, and to Brenna Darling and Bethany Nauert for bringing this book to life. Thank you also to the team at Clarkson Potter and our agent Eve Attermann.

Tastemade Team

Lily Ng

Tyler Wildermuth

Daniel Kesner

Sarah Anne Bargatze

Kathy Jacobsen

Anne-Marie Kabia

Justin Raths

James Veitch

Megahn Perry

Sarah Beaumont

Michela Newhouse

Jeremy Strauss

Emma Henkrikson

Julz Rochce

Ria Thirkul

John Acosta

Ben Grecko

Savanah Joekle

Coty Walker

Dan D'Agostino

Jonathan Davis

Amanda Dameron

Nathan Rea

Pollyanna Jacobs

Casey Gerber

Weekend Refresh Episode Designers

Brenna Darling

Meg Savage

Heather Knight-Wilcock

Michelle Villemaire

Jason Lai

Samantha Santana

Julie Khuu

Ciara Perez

Jay Montepare

Clarkson Potter Team

Angelin Adams

Darian Keels

Gabrielle Van Tassel

Jennifer K. Beal Davis

Mia Johnson

Kelli Tokos

Patricia Shaw

Christine Tanigawa

Francis Lam

Aaron Wehner

page
162

Index

also available

Clarkson Potter/Publishers
New York